Telecourse Guide
for

United States Government

Second Edition

Telecourse Guide
for

United States Government

Second Edition

EILEEN LYNCH
LINDA CAMP KEITH
SUE LEE

Telecourse Guide revised by
TED LEWIS

Produced by:

DALLAS TeleLearning
Dallas County Community College District

In cooperation with

Australia • Canada • Mexico • Singapore • Spain • United Kingdom • United States

Assistant Chancellor/LeCroy Center:	Pamela K. Quinn
Executive Dean, Distance Education:	Jacquelyn B. Tulloch
National Government Content Specialist:	Eileen Lynch
Co-authors:	Linda Camp Keith and Sue Lee
Project Editor:	Linda Condos
Producer:	Julia Dyer
Producer's Assistant:	Debra Brown
Senior Instructional Designer:	Nora Coto Busby
Associate Dean, Distance Education:	Michael Dennehy
Telecommunications Information Specialist:	Evelyn J. Wong

ISBN: 0-15-507005-3

COPYRIGHT © 2002 Wadsworth, a division of Thomson Learning, Inc. Thomson Learning ™ is a trademark used herein under license.

ALL RIGHTS RESERVED. No part of this work covered by the copyright hereon may be reproduced or used in any form or by any means — graphic, electronic, or mechanical, including photocopying, recording, taping, Web distribution, or information storage or retrieval systems — without the written permission of the publisher.

Wadsworth Group/Thomson Learning
10 Davis Drive
Belmont CA 94002-3098
USA

For information about our products, contact us:
Thomson Learning Academic Resource Center
1-800-423-0563
http://www.wadsworth.com

For permission to use material from this text, contact us by
Web: http://www.thomsonrights.com
Fax: 1-800-730-2215
Phone: 1-800-730-2214

Printed in the United States of America
10 9 8 7 6 5 4 3

Contents

To You, the Student	vi
Telecourse Organization	vii
Telecourse Guidelines	ix

Lessons	Page
1. Democratic Voices in a Changing Society	1
2. The Living Constitution	11
3. Constitution in Crisis	21
4. Federalism	29
5. Intergovernmental Relations	37
6. Public Opinion and Political Socialization	45
7. Participation in Democracy	53
8. Mass Media and Government	61
9. Interest Groups	69
10. Political Parties	79
11. Media and Elections	91
12. Presidential Elections	97
13. Congressional Elections	107
14. Congress	115
15. Legislative Process	123
16. Congress and the President	129
17. The Presidency	135
18. Bureaucracy	145
19. Domestic Policy	153
20. Foreign Policy	163
21. Global Politics	173
22. Federal Courts	181
23. Criminal Justice	189
24. Due Process of Law	197
25. First Amendment Freedoms	205
26. The Struggle for Equal Rights	215

Contributors	225

To You, the Student

Our democratic government may seem chaotic and confusing because we are living in a rapidly changing society. How do we solve our problems of crime and air pollution, or keep our food safe, our planes flying, and the economy secure? Do our actions in the political arena make any difference? Do our representatives listen to us? How can we be more effective analysts and citizens?

Beyond our daily lives, how does our government affect the rest of the world? Are we really living in a global village? Does what we do affect the rest of the world? Are we, as citizens in a democracy, living up to that model?

Voices in Democracy will explore these and other questions relating to our United States government institutions, politics, and policy.

In the video programs, we explore contemporary issues as examples of our government in action. This approach means that *Voices in Democracy*, as the title suggests, is citizen-activist oriented. By focusing on contemporary issues we try to bring political participation and political action into the classroom.

If you have any suggestions for improvement in any aspect of this course, you can contact me at the R. Jan LeCroy Center for Educational Telecommunications, 9596 Walnut Street, Dallas, TX 75243-2112.

—Eileen Lynch
Content Specialist

Telecourse Organization

Voices in Democracy: United States Government is designed as a comprehensive learning system consisting of three elements: telecourse guide, textbook, and video programs.

TELECOURSE GUIDE

The telecourse guide for this course is:

Lynch, Eileen, Linda Camp Keith, and Sue Lee. *Telecourse Guide for Voices in Democracy: United States Government.* 2nd Edition. Fort Worth, Texas: Harcourt College Publishers, 2001. ISBN: 0-15-507005-3.

No course functions effectively without a knowledgeable professor. The professor is an indispensable part of any learning experience, including a telecourse. The telecourse guide directs the student between contacts with the professor. It provides students with assignments, describes learning objectives and web activities, and provides practice tests. The telecourse guide is the student's pilot or tutor through the course.

Development of the student telecourse guide included work by an instructional design specialist and a content specialist. Each lesson contains a lesson assignment, an overview, a lesson goal, textbook objectives, video objectives, practice test questions, and answers to provide feedback to the student before formal testing. In addition, the appendix contains the names of contributors to this course. The practice tests are directly related to lesson objectives. If you follow the recommendations in the telecourse guide and carefully view each video program, you should be able to successfully accomplish all of the requirements for this course.

TEXTBOOK

In addition to the telecourse guide, a textbook is required for this course:

Cummings, Milton C., Jr., and David Wise. *Democracy Under Pressure: An Introduction to the American Political System*. 9th Ed. Fort Worth, Texas: Harcourt College Publishers, 2001. ISBN: 0-15-507002-9.

The textbook provides essential and interesting information about the government and politics of this nation. Specific reading assignments for each lesson appear in the telecourse guide at the beginning of the lesson. Be sure to read this material before viewing the video program.

VIDEO PROGRAMS

The video series for this course is:

Voices in Democracy: United States Government.

The course includes twenty-six video programs, one for each of the twenty-six telecourse guide lessons. Each video program is correlated with the telecourse guide and the lesson assignment for that lesson. The student should read the video objectives in the telecourse guide before watching the program.
    If the programs are broadcast more than once in your area, or if video or audio tapes are available at your college, students might find it helpful to watch the video programs more than once or to listen to an audio tape for review. Students should be encouraged to record the video programs for subsequent study and review.

TELECOURSE PLUS

An online interactive option is available to students whose institutions have opted to license the course. The web activities are useful for working with "real-time" information related to the lesson content and objectives. If your course includes this PLUS component, please contact your instructor for the course website address and required password.

Telecourse Guidelines

Follow these guidelines as you study the material presented in each lesson:

1. LESSON ASSIGNMENT—
   Review the Lesson Assignment in order to schedule your time appropriately. Pay careful attention; the titles and numbers of the textbook chapter, the telecourse guide lesson, and the video program may be different from one another.

2. OVERVIEW—
   Read the Overview for an introduction to the lesson material.

3. TEXTBOOK OBJECTIVES—
   To get the most from your reading, review the Textbook Objectives, then read the assignment. You may want to write responses or notes to reinforce what you have learned.

4. VIDEO OBJECTIVES—
   To get the most from the video segment of the lesson, review the Video Objectives, then watch the video. You may want to write responses or notes to reinforce what you have learned.

5. WEB RESOURCE PAGE—
   gln.dcccd.edu/usagovernment
   The web resource links are provided for enrichment of the basic course content, and may be used by your instructor as experiential learning exercises.

6. PRACTICE TEST—
   After reading the assignment, watching the video, and addressing the objectives, you should be able to complete the following Practice Test. Some essay questions in this Practice Test may be included in your exams. When you have completed the Practice Test, turn to the Answer Key to score your answers.

7. ANSWER KEY—
    The following provides the answers and references for the Practice Test questions. Objectives are referenced using the following abbreviations:
    T=Textbook Objectives   V=Video Objectives

Lesson 1

Democratic Voices in a Changing Society

LESSON ASSIGNMENTS

Review the following assignments in order to schedule your time appropriately. Pay careful attention. The titles and numbers of the textbook chapter, the telecourse guide lesson, and the video program may be different from one another.

Text:

    Cummings and Wise, *Democracy Under Pressure,* Chapter 1, "Government and People," pp. 3–27.

Video:

    "Democratic Voices in a Changing Society" from the series *Voices in Democracy: United States Government.*

Activities:

    One or more activities may be assigned to this lesson. Refer to your syllabus.

OVERVIEW

This lesson examines the relationship between government and the people. One of the important philosophical debates of the 2000 presidential election involved the proper role of government in society. In the United States, the government has a broad impact on the lives of its citizens, and in return citizens have numerous ways in which they may influence their government. Since we live in a representative democracy we may participate in the election of those persons that represent us. We may also participate in interest groups and through forms of direct action, such as protests and demonstrations. Our government may be thought of as a political system that processes our demands, actions, and feedback into political outputs or public policies. The United States has experienced many changes in the last few decades that have altered the face of national politics and the perceptions we have of our abilities as a nation. We will continue to face important social, economic, and technological changes, and we will be faced with the question of what role the government should or can play in addressing these issues, and we will be asked what we as participants in a democracy can do.

LESSON GOAL

You should be able to understand the relationship between government, politics, and power in the U.S. democracy and the roles that people can play to affect policy and action.

TEXTBOOK OBJECTIVES

The following objectives are designed to help you get the most from the text. Review them before reading the assignment. You may want to write notes to reinforce what you have learned.

1. Discuss the 2000 presidential election, particularly the philosophical differences of the Bush and Gore campaigns in regard to the role of government.

2. Explore the new questions facing U.S. citizens, given the changes in the political environment and in the perceptions of us.

3. Examine the breadth of the impact of government on the average citizen's life.

4. Discuss how citizens may have an impact on government by voting in elections and by participating in party activities and interest groups. Also discuss how citizens influence government through public opinion and through direct action, such as protests and demonstrations.

5. Define and explore the relationship between government, politics, democracy, and power.

6. Discuss the difference between our system of representative democracy and a direct democracy. Examine how concepts of majority rule and equality fit within our system of democracy.

7. Describe the major elements of Easton's concept of the political system and explain how they relate to the system's production of binding decisions.

8. Define *public policymaking*. Identify the key components of public policy analysis and describe how these components may be used to evaluate government and politics.

9. Discuss the impact on U.S. society that has occurred or may occur due to the changing demographic makeup of the population and due to major technological, economic, and social changes.

10. Assess the ability of our system of government to deal with these changes as we begin the twenty-first century.

VIDEO OBJECTIVES

The following objectives are designed to help you get the most from the video segment of this lesson. Review them before watching the video. You may want to write notes to reinforce what you have learned.

11. Explain how people in a representative democracy can gain power to effect change.

12. Explain the role of media in providing timely information for people in a democracy.

13. Analyze some of the issues that the U.S. political system will probably face in the twenty-first century.

PRACTICE TEST

After reading the assignment, watching the video, and addressing the objectives, you should be able to complete the following Practice Test. Some essay questions in this Practice Test may be included in your exams. When you have completed the Practice Test, turn to the Answer Key to score your answers.

MULTIPLE CHOICE

Select the single best answer. If more than one answer is required, it will be so indicated.

1. Which of the following is true of the 2000 presidential race between George W. Bush and Al Gore?
   A. Al Gore did not distance himself from Bill Clinton, and he defended Clinton's transgressions.
   B. George W. Bush favored enacting new gun control laws as well as enforcing existing ones.
   C. George W. Bush proposed to sign a bill banning "partial-birth abortions" and to lead the country toward a culture that values "the life of the unborn."
   D. All of the above.

2. Which of the following was a result of the 2000 election?
   A. Republicans retained both houses of Congress.
   B. Democrats gained control of the House of Representatives.
   C. Democrats and Republicans were equally divided in the House of Representatives.
   D. Democrats and Republicans were equally divided in the Senate.

3. Which of the following is a change that occurred in U.S. politics by the early 1990s?
   A. Special interest groups, often well-financed and supporting single issues, had declined as actors in the nation's politics.
   B. The nation's political parties appeared to be declining in importance, and public confidence in the institutions of government was relatively low.
   C. There had been a decrease in the importance of political action committees (PACs).
   D. All of the above.

4. In the United States, government is extraordinarily _____
   A. simple.
   B. complicated.
   C. vague.
   D. detached.

5. The American system of government is based on the concept that power flows from _____
   A. the government to the people.
   B. the federal government to the state governments and then to the people.
   C. the people to the government.
   D. the Bill of Rights to the state governments.

6. When one utilizes confrontation and other disruptive actions such as "sit-ins" to achieve political ends, one is participating in _____
   A. direct action.
   B. an interest group.
   C. apartheid.
   D. a political party.

7. The individuals, institutions, and processes that make the rules for a society and possess the power to enforce those rules are _____
   A. democracy.
   B. direct action.
   C. government.
   D. feedback.

8. "The pursuit and exercise of power" is the definition of _____
   A. government.
   B. output.
   C. politics.
   D. *demos*.

9. The government of the United States is considered to be _____
   A. a direct democracy.
   B. an aristocracy.
   C. a unitary democracy.
   D. a representative democracy.

10. Demands of a political system _____
    A. are the attitudes and actions of people that sustain and buttress the political system.
    B. describe the positive responses of the rest of society to the decisions made by the authorities in a political system.
    C. are chiefly the binding decisions made by the political system.
    D. are what people and groups want from the system.

11. Inputs of a political system are _____
    A. the product of output and feedback.
    B. the product of demands and output.
    C. the product of supports and feedback.
    D. the product of demands and supports.

12. A course of action that is shaped by government officials is _____
    A. feedback.
    B. a demand.
    C. a support.
    D. public policy.

13. When we are analyzing public policy, "distribution" is _____
    A. determining the subjects that public officials deal with.
    B. the course of action decided upon by the government.
    C. the actions taken by government to carry out a policy.
    D. concern with the question of who wins and who loses from a given public policy.

14. Which of the following is correct regarding recent population shifts in the United States?
    A. The importance of the "farm bloc" decreased.
    B. California surpassed New York as the most populous state in the Union.
    C. Since World War II, as African Americans migrated to northern cities, many whites moved to the suburbs.
    D. All of the above.

15. In the early 1960s, African Americans influenced changes that came about because of _____
    A. past discriminations.
    B. legislative mandates.
    C. economic injustices.
    D. citizen activism.

16. The Southern Poverty Law Center was founded in 1971 primarily to _____
    A. confront the causes of poverty in the South.
    B. take on litigation following laws passed during the civil rights movement.
    C. provide free legal counsel for those on welfare.
    D. give new minority attorneys a chance to practice law.

17. The man who in the mid-1960s organized the migrant farm workers in California into a union called the United Farm Workers was _____
    A. Cesar Romero.
    B. Henry Cisneros.
    C. Pancho Medrano.
    D. Cesar Chavez.

18. CNN believes that to keep people informed with a full, fair breadth of viewpoints, they need to provide _____
    A. liberal and conservative views.
    B. many different foreign viewpoints.
    C. all kinds of views on particular events.
    D. all of the above.

19. Arthur Schlesinger, Jr. believes that the most important issue facing the U.S. government today in domestic affairs is quite simply _____
    A. race.
    B. money.
    C. welfare.
    D. health care.

ESSAY/PROBLEM QUESTIONS

20. Define the terms *government*, *politics*, *power*, and *democracy*. Discuss the difference between representative democracy and direct democracy and evaluate how these terms relate to democracy in the United States.

21. Describe three ways in which government has an impact on the people of the United States and three ways in which the people of the United States may have an impact on the government. How are these types of influence limited or enhanced by the representative government, majority rule, equality, and constitutional government?

22. Your textbook concludes the chapter by discussing population, social, and technological changes that affect our society and politics. Evaluate how well you think our political system will be able to deal with each of these types of changes.

23. Describe and analyze some of the political action that people have used to bring about change in the United States. What do you think is the most effective way to participate? Explain.

24. What seem to be the issues that affect the general attitude of the U.S. public toward the future? What do you think is the most important issue facing our government for the twenty-first century?

ANSWER KEY

The following provides the answers and references for the Practice Test questions. Objectives are referenced using the following abbreviations:

T=Textbook Objectives   V=Video Objectives

1.	D	T1	Cummings, pp. 4–5
2.	A	T1	Cummings, p. 4
3.	B	T2	Cummings, pp. 6–8
4.	B	T3	Cummings, p. 10
5.	C	T4	Cummings, pp. 11–12
6.	A	T4	Cummings, p. 13
7.	C	T5	Cummings, p. 16
8.	C	T5	Cummings, pp. 16–17
9.	D	T6	Cummings, p. 15
10.	D	T7	Cummings, p. 17
11.	D	T7	Cummings, p. 17
12.	D	T8	Cummings, p. 17
13.	D	T8	Cummings, p. 18
14.	D	T9	Cummings, pp. 20–21
15.	D	V11	Video
16.	B	V11	Video
17.	D	V11	Video
18.	D	V12	Video
19.	A	V13	Video
20.		T5, T6	Cummings, pp. 14–16
21.		T6	Cummings, pp. 10–13
22.		T9, T10	Cummings, pp. 18–25
23.		V11	Video
24.		V13	Video

Lesson 1—Democratic Voices in a Changing Society

Lesson 2

The Living Constitution

LESSON ASSIGNMENTS

Review the following assignments in order to schedule your time appropriately. Pay careful attention. The titles and numbers of the textbook chapter, the telecourse guide lesson, and the video program may be different from one another.

Text:
> Cummings and Wise, *Democracy Under Pressure,* Chapter 2, "The Constitutional Framework," pp. 29–57.

Video:
> "The Living Constitution" from the series *Voices in Democracy: United States Government.*

Activities:
> One or more activities may be assigned to this lesson. Refer to your syllabus.

OVERVIEW

This lesson examines the origins and political foundations of the U.S. Constitution. It explores how our early experiences under colonial rule and our first attempt at self-government under the Articles of Confederation shaped the form of government we eventually chose. Several debates erupted as we tried to frame and ratify a national constitution. These debates are discussed, as are the motives of the framers. Key constitutional concepts such as federalism, separation of power, checks and balances, and judicial review are examined in light of their relation to each other and to democratic governance. The individual sections and provisions of the completed Constitution and its subsequent amendments are described. To examine whether the U.S. Constitution is a living document, the expansion of the commerce clause through interpretation and law exemplifies the changes as society has changed. The amendment process is used to show that the Constitution has become a more inclusive document to represent all people in the United States.

LESSON GOAL

You should understand that the U.S. Constitution is a living document, as it is interpreted and changed to reflect the conditions of the times throughout history.

TEXTBOOK OBJECTIVES

The following objectives are designed to help you get the most from the text. Review them before reading the assignment. You may want to write notes to reinforce what you have learned.

1. Examine the extent to which constitutional government affects life in the United States as illustrated by recent Supreme Court cases.

2. Examine the origins and political foundation of the U.S. Declaration of Independence and Constitution.

3. Describe the colonial governments under which the thirteen colonies lived and explain the paradox of American colonial experience.

4. Evaluate the flaws of the Articles of Confederation as a system of government and discuss the specific problems related to changing the system.

5. Describe the controversies and compromises that emerged in the writing of the Constitution and identify the opposing viewpoints on the ratification of the Constitution.

6. Describe the key components of our political system and how they relate to each other: federalism, separation of powers, checks and balances, judicial review.

7. Explain how the Supreme Court in the case of *Marbury v. Madison* established the power of judicial review.

8. Evaluate the argument that the framers of the Constitution were men of great wealth and power who had a vested interest in limiting democratic rights.

9. Identify and briefly describe the processes of nation building that Seymour Martin Lipset describes.

10. Identify the basic powers which are given to each of the three branches in the main articles of the Constitution. Describe the amendment process, the Bill of Rights, and the later amendments to the Constitution.

11. Evaluate whether the constitutional framework that was constructed in 1787 is flexible enough to meet the needs of our complex society and the needs of the twenty-first century.

VIDEO OBJECTIVES

The following objectives are designed to help you get the most from the video segment of this lesson. Review them before watching the video. You may want to write notes to reinforce what you have learned.

12. List the major components and principles of the U.S. Constitution and explain how they contribute to the concept of a "living document."

13. Explain the debate that has developed over the interpretation of the Constitution's commerce clause.

14. Discuss the importance of the Bill of Rights in today's society.

15. Describe the hurdles that have challenged the United States as an inclusive nation. Use the women's movement as an example.

16. Explain how the right to privacy has challenged and continues to challenge the interpretation of the U.S. Constitution.

PRACTICE TEST

After reading the assignment, watching the video, and addressing the objectives, you should be able to complete the following Practice Test. Some essay questions in this Practice Test may be included in your exams. When you have completed the Practice Test, turn to the Answer Key to score your answers.

MULTIPLE CHOICE

Select the single best answer. If more than one answer is required, it will be so indicated.

1. Based upon recent Supreme Court interpretation of the U.S. Constitution, we have seen which of the following constitutional limitations placed on society?
   A. Public school officials may forbid a Bible study club from being part of a school's extracurricular program.
   B. State legislatures and Congress may pass laws that make it a crime to burn a U.S. flag in protest.
   C. Officially supported segregation in public schools is unconstitutional.
   D. Forced school desegregation is unconstitutional.

2. After Congress adopted the resolution that declared the colonies' independence from Great Britain, Congress selected which of the following persons to write a justification for that action?
   A. Thomas Jefferson
   B. Thomas Paine
   C. James Madison
   D. Richard Henry Lee

3. Which of the following was a grievance that the colonists voiced against England?
   A. They had no representation in the English Parliament.
   B. They resented and disputed London's right to raise revenue in the colonies.
   C. England placed tight restrictions on colonial trade and provided protections for producers in England.
   D. All of the above.

4. Which of the following statements describes a weakness of the Articles of Confederation?
   A. Congress had the power to levy taxes.
   B. The president was powerful relative to Congress.
   C. The Articles could be amended only by unanimous consent of the states.
   D. There were too many national courts.

5. How were the Virginia and New Jersey plans different?
   A. The New Jersey plan would have just amended the Articles of Confederation.
   B. The Virginia plan proposed an entirely new constitution.
   C. The New Jersey plan would have left the national government weak.
   D. All of the above.

6. Which of the following is true regarding the convention that met in Philadelphia in 1787?
   A. The delegates were relatively young.
   B. The delegates generally were men of wealth and influence.
   C. The sessions were held in secret.
   D. All of the above.

7. The Connecticut Plan provided for which of the following?
   A. A House of Representatives apportioned by the number of free inhabitants plus three-fifths of the slaves and a Senate consisting of two members from each state selected by the state legislatures
   B. A House of Representatives apportioned by the number of free inhabitants and a Senate consisting of two members from each state selected by the state legislatures
   C. A House of Representatives apportioned by the number of free inhabitants plus three-fifths of the slaves and a Senate consisting of two members from each state elected directly by the people of those states
   D. A bicameral legislature in which both houses would be apportioned according to the number of free inhabitants plus three-fifths of the slaves

8. The power of judicial review is explicitly granted to the Supreme Court in which article of the Constitution?
   A. Article I
   B. Article II
   C. Article III
   D. None of the above

9. Under Article II the president _____
   A. has the power to make treaties with the advice and consent of two-thirds of the Senate.
   B. has the power to appoint judges, ambassadors, and other high officials with Senate approval.
   C. is designated the Commander-in-Chief of the armed forces.
   D. all of the above.

10. Which of the following amendments granted the right to vote to segments of the population that had formerly been denied this privilege?
    A. Fifteenth Amendment
    B. Nineteenth Amendment
    C. Twenty-sixth Amendment
    D. All of the above

11. In *Marbury v. Madison*, Chief Justice John Marshall argued that _____
    A. Congress has the power to determine for itself whether the laws it makes are constitutional.
    B. the Supreme Court has the power to determine what laws are constitutional.
    C. the Constitution was not superior to an act of Congress.
    D. the Supreme Court did not have the power of judicial review.

12. Which of the following best describes the delegates who met in Philadelphia to propose amendments to the Articles of Confederation?
    A. They were generally small farmers and artisans.
    B. They were generally laborers and small farmers.
    C. They were generally men of wealth and influence.
    D. They represented all segments of the population of the United States.

13. Seymour Martin Lipset has observed that _____
    A. The United States proceeded easily toward the establishment of democratic political institutions.
    B. The process of nation building in the United States was quick and easy.
    C. It was initially touch and go whether the United States would survive as an entity.
    D. All of the above

14. Which of the following powers was granted to Congress in Article I of the Constitution?
    A. The power to regulate commerce
    B. The power to pass bills of attainder
    C. The power to pass ex post facto laws
    D. All of the above

15. What happened to the proposed constitutional amendment to balance the federal budget in 1995?
    A. It passed the House.
    B. The president was opposed to it.
    C. It failed to pass the Senate.
    D. All of the above.

16. The writers of the U.S. Constitution drew their inspiration from American sources and from _____
    A. early written constitutions.
    B. European thinkers.
    C. Roman documents.
    D. the writings of Aristotle.

17. Judicial review is the principle which caused President Woodrow Wilson to call the Supreme Court _____
    A. a dictator of U.S. government.
    B. a constitutional convention in continuous session.
    C. a divider of the unity of the states.
    D. none of the above.

Lesson 2—The Living Constitution

18. John Marshall interpreted interstate commerce as _____
    A. travel from one contiguous country to another.
    B. shipping from one contiguous country to another.
    C. intercourse that passes through state lines.
    D. intercourse between companies within a state.

19. The Bill of Rights to the Constitution was added to guarantee _____
    A. judicial review.
    B. the checks and balances system.
    C. the rights of individuals.
    D. the rights of the states.

20. One of the methods of making the U.S. Constitution more inclusive has been _____
    A. affirmative action.
    B. the amendment process.
    C. the freedom of peaceful assembly.
    D. the appellate process.

21. Many of the constitutional issues the United States faces today concern _____
    A. the right to privacy.
    B. expansion of the state governments' control.
    C. the increase in crime.
    D. the rights of welfare recipients.

ESSAY/PROBLEM QUESTIONS

22. What were the chief weaknesses of the government under the Articles of Confederation? Describe the ways in which our current constitution was an improvement over the Articles of Confederation. Evaluate whether the current constitutional framework is flexible enough to meet the needs of our complex society. Be sure to give examples to support your evaluation.

23. Identify which specific articles of the Constitution outline the main powers and duties of the president, Congress, and the judiciary. Give two examples of the powers or duties dealt with in each of the three articles.

24. Although written more than two hundred years ago, the U.S. Constitution is still referred to as a "living document." Explain what this term "living document" means in your essay.

25. The principles of interstate commerce, privacy, and equality have been interpreted or added as a part of the U.S. Constitution. Give examples to justify your essay.

ANSWER KEY

The following provides the answers and references for the Practice Test questions. Objectives are referenced using the following abbreviations:

T=Textbook Objectives   V=Video Objectives

#	Ans	Obj	Reference
1.	C	T1	Cummings, pp. 30–31
2.	A	T2	Cummings, p. 32
3.	D	T3	Cummings, p. 37
4.	C	T4	Cummings, p. 38
5.	D	T5	Cummings, pp. 40–41
6.	D	T5, V15	Cummings, pp. 39–40, Video
7.	A	T5	Cummings, p. 41
8.	D	T6, V12	Cummings, p. 45, Video
9.	D	T6	Cummings, p. 49
10.	D	T6, V15	Cummings, pp. 51–53, Video
11.	B	T7, V12	Cummings, p. 45, Video
12.	C	T8	Cummings, pp. 39–40
13.	C	T9	Cummings, pp. 47–48
14.	A	T10	Cummings, p. 48
15.	D	T10	Cummings, p. 53
16.	B	V12	Video
17.	B	V12	Video
18.	C	V13	Video
19.	C	V14	Video
20.	B	V15	Video
21.	A	V16	Video
22.		T4, T10, T11	Cummings, pp. 37–47
23.		T10	Cummings, pp. 48–49, pp. A5–A7
24.		V12	Video
25.		V15	Video

Lesson 3

Constitution in Crisis

LESSON ASSIGNMENTS

Review the following assignments in order to schedule your time appropriately. Pay careful attention. The titles and numbers of the textbook chapter, the telecourse guide lesson, and the video program may be different from one another.

Text:
>Cummings and Wise, *Democracy Under Pressure,* Chapter 13, "The President," pp. 440–442 ("The Watergate Scandal: A President Resigns"), Chapter 13, "The President," pp. 442–446 ("Presidential Impeachment, Disability, and Succession"), and Chapter 5, "The Struggle for Equal Rights," pp. 151–152 ("The Case of Linda Carol Brown" through "Little Rock, Oxford, and Alabama").

Video:
>"Constitution in Crisis" from the series *Voices in Democracy: United States Government.*

Activities:
>One or more activities may be assigned to this lesson. Refer to your syllabus.

OVERVIEW

This lesson examines several constitutional crises: the Civil War, the Watergate scandal, the Clinton Scandal, the implementation of the Supreme Court's *Brown v. Board of Education* decision that called for the desegregation of public schools, and a president's assassination. These sections also examine the ability of our constitutionally structured system to deal effectively with such crises. In this lesson, you will evaluate the role the president, the Congress, and the Supreme Court each played in resolving these crises. A constitutional crisis resolution promotes the continued importance of the Constitution in our democracy during changing times.

LESSON GOAL

You should be able to explain the challenges the U.S. Constitution has weathered during crisis situations.

TEXTBOOK OBJECTIVES

The following objectives are designed to help you get the most from the text. Review them before reading the assignment. You may want to write notes to reinforce what you have learned.

1. Examine the events that became known as Watergate. Identify the key players and the illegal or unethical activities that were disclosed during the inquiry into the break-in.

2. Examine the role of Congress in the investigation of Watergate and the convictions that followed.

3. Describe the role the Supreme Court played in the investigation.

4. Discuss the constitutional and historical origins of impeachment.

5. Discuss and evaluate the impeachment proceedings for President Nixon.

6. Examine the scandal that led to the impeachment of Bill Clinton.

7. Compare the Clinton scandal with the Nixon scandal in terms of abuse of power.

8. Describe the constitutional crisis that arises when a president is incapacitated and how the Twenty-fifth Amendment addresses it.

9. Describe the case of *Brown v. Board of Education of Topeka, Kansas* and its impact on school segregation.

10. Evaluate the problems in implementing Supreme Court decisions such as the *Brown* decision.

11. Discuss the constitutional crisis that developed in integrating Little Rock's Central High School and various southern universities.

12. Evaluate the effectiveness of our constitutional structure to deal with crises such as Watergate and the southern reaction to *Brown*.

VIDEO OBJECTIVES

The following objectives are designed to help you get the most from the video segment of this lesson. Review them before watching the video. You may want to write notes to reinforce what you have learned.

13. Explain the role the U.S. Constitution played before and following the Civil War.

14. Explain the challenge that school integration in Little Rock, Arkansas, in 1957 presented to the U.S. Constitution and the nation.

15. Describe the constitutional crisis that arose when President Kennedy was assassinated and how the Twenty-fifth Amendment resolved it.

16. Describe the constitutional roles of each branch of government in resolving the Watergate crisis.

PRACTICE TEST

After reading the assignment, watching the video, and addressing the objectives, you should be able to complete the following Practice Test. Some essay questions in this Practice Test may be included in your exams. When you have completed the Practice Test, turn to the Answer Key to score your answers.

MULTIPLE CHOICE

Select the single best answer. If more than one answer is required, it will be so indicated.

1. Which of the following was NOT later revealed about the Watergate break-in?
   A. Several of the burglars had worked for the CIA.
   B. The break-in had not been ordered by anyone high up in the Nixon administration.
   C. The break-in had been financed by money from the Republican party.
   D. The burglars had "bugged" the offices they broke into, and reports of the conversations were delivered to the president's reelection committee.

2. What was the role of Congress during the investigation of the Watergate scandal?
   A. The Senate formed a select committee to hold hearings.
   B. The Senate appointed a special prosecutor to investigate the Watergate case.
   C. The Senate Republicans remained loyal to the president all the way.
   D. All of the above.

3. Which of the following statements accurately describes the impeachment process?
   A. Only the House can bring impeachment charges against the president.
   B. The president may be impeached by Congress and removed from office.
   C. The Senate hears and decides impeachment cases.
   D. All of the above.

4. Bill Clinton was impeached by the United States House of Representatives on the grounds of _____
   A. "improper sexual relationship."
   B. "abuse of federal power."
   C. "accepting illegal campaign contributions."
   D. "preventing, obstructing, and impeding the administration of justice."

5. In *Brown v. Board of Education of Topeka, Kansas* the Supreme Court _____
   A. ruled that the Fifteenth Amendment guarantee of equal protection of the law applied in this case.
   B. ruled that the "separate but equal doctrine" was unconstitutional.
   C. ruled that public schools could be segregated if the facilities were equal.
   D. ruled that only tangible factors were considered when determining whether schools were equal.

6. What was the reaction in the South *to Brown v. Board of Education*?
   A. Massive compliance
   B. Slow but steady compliance
   C. Compliance only after being forced by troops called out by the president
   D. Compliance only after being forced by troops called out by the Supreme Court

7. In which of the following cases did the U.S. Supreme Court rule that Congress had no power to exclude slavery from any of the territories of the United States?
   A. *Marbury v. Madison*
   B. *Scott v. Sanford*
   C. *Plessy v. Ferguson*
   D. *Brown v. Board of Education*

8. Initially, according to Craig Rains (a white student), the Little Rock situation was a _____
   A. states rights versus the federal government issue.
   B. states rights versus a public school board issue.
   C. federal government versus the people issue.
   D. people versus a public school board issue.

9. Which of the following is NOT a step in filling the vacant office of vice president?
   A. The president nominates a new vice president.
   B. The nominee will take office if confirmed.
   C. The Supreme Court must approve the credentials of the nominee.
   D. The House and Senate must approve the nominee in a majority vote.

10. The Watergate case raised two constitutional questions: one was whether the president is subject to judicial process, and two was whether the presidential tapes were covered by what is known as _____
    A. executive agreement.
    B. executive privilege.
    C. presidential exemption.
    D. judicial executive.

ESSAY/PROBLEM QUESTIONS

11. List the illegal and unethical activities that were a part of the Watergate scandal. Who were the key players in the illegal activities involved in the Watergate scandal? What was the relationship of each player to the president?

12. Describe the complete impeachment process and the role played by the Senate, the House, and the Supreme Court in this process. Evaluate their effectiveness in dealing with the crisis.

13. Discuss ways in which the Watergate scandal and the school integration battle in Little Rock could turn into potential constitutional crises. Evaluate whether our constitutional structure was able to deal with the events efficiently.

14. Describe the major steps in filling the vacant office of the vice president, and explain how it has been used.

15. Describe the problems that surrounded the Watergate affair. Explain the usefulness of understanding the abuse of power.

ANSWER KEY

The following provides the answers and references for the Practice Test questions. Objectives are referenced using the following abbreviations:

T=Textbook Objectives V=Video Objectives

1. B .... T1 .... Cummings, p. 440
2. A .... T2 .... Cummings, pp. 441–442
3. D .... T4 .... Cummings, p. 442
4. D .... T6, T7 .... Cummings, p. 444
5. B .... T9 .... Cummings, p. 151
6. C .... T10 .... Cummings, pp. 151–152
7. B .... V13 .... Video
8. A .... V14 .... Video
9. C .... V15 .... Video
10. B .... V16 .... Video
11. .... T1 .... Cummings, pp. 440–443
12. .... T2, T3, T12 .... Cummings, pp. 442–444
13. .... T10, T11, T12 .... Cummings, pp. 440-443, pp. 151–152
14. .... V12 .... Video
15. .... V13 .... Video

Lesson 4

Federalism

LESSON ASSIGNMENTS

Review the following assignments in order to schedule your time appropriately. Pay careful attention. The titles and numbers of the textbook chapter, the telecourse guide lesson, and the video program may be different from one another.

Text:
    Cummings and Wise, *Democracy Under Pressure,* Chapter 3, "The Federal System," pp. 59–85.

Video:
    "Federalism" from the series *Voices in Democracy: United States Government.*

Activities:
    One or more activities may be assigned to this lesson. Refer to your syllabus.

OVERVIEW

This lesson examines the U.S. system of federalism: its advantages and disadvantages, its different faces over various periods of time, and its impact on U.S. governance and politics. The chapter also examines the tension and conflict between the national and state governments that is created by the system. Finally, the chapter explores the relationship between federalism, federal and state spending, and the size of government. In the video, federalism is examined as it functions using varied examples of conflict and cooperation between the national government and the state governments when solving problems.

LESSON GOAL

Explain the balance of power question that federalism created and list some of the conflicts that have occurred over the last two hundred years.

TEXTBOOK OBJECTIVES

The following objectives are designed to help you get the most from the text. Review them before reading the assignment. You may want to write notes to reinforce what you have learned.

1. Explain the meaning of the concept of federalism in the context of the United States. Distinguish between unitary and federal systems of government.

2. Identify and evaluate the advantages and disadvantages of the system of federalism in the United States.

3. Identify and distinguish among the different faces that federalism has manifested over the course of our history: dual federalism, cooperative federalism, creative federalism, new federalism, and regulatory federalism.

4. Describe the tension between the federal and state governments that has developed as a result of regulatory federalism and unfunded mandates.

5. Identify the powers and the limitations of the states under the Constitution.

6. Define and distinguish between *enumerated powers*, *implied powers*, *inherent powers*, and *concurrent powers*.

7. Explain how state actions are limited by the supremacy clause and how interstate obligations are controlled by the Constitution, especially in regard to the concepts in the full faith and credit clause, full privileges and immunities clause, and interstate compacts.

8. Analyze the impact of federalism on governance in the United States. Identify the ways in which federalism affects state spending and evaluate its impact on the states.

9. Evaluate the ability of a federal system to adapt to the needs of the next century.

VIDEO OBJECTIVES

The following objectives are designed to help you get the most from the video segment of this lesson. Review them before watching the video. You may want to write notes to reinforce what you have learned.

10. Explain the balance of power question that federalism created, and list some of the conflicts that have occurred over the last two hundred years.

11. Explain the role federalism plays in addressing the national transportation issue.

12. Discuss the question of federalism following the bombing of the federal building in Oklahoma City.

13. Explain the problem immigration presents for federalism.

PRACTICE TEST

After reading the assignment, watching the video, and addressing the objectives, you should be able to complete the following Practice Test. Some essay questions in this Practice Test may be included in your exams. When you have completed the Practice Test, turn to the Answer Key to score your answers.

MULTIPLE CHOICE

Select the single best answer. If more than one answer is required, it will be so indicated.

1. A state that is administered by a government that is centralized and whose policies such as education are set by the central government is _____
   A. a unitary state.
   B. a federal state.
   C. a confederal state.
   D. none of the above.

2. Those who favor federalism argue that _____
   A. it permits more opportunities for political participation.
   B. it allows special interests to frustrate efforts to solve national problems.
   C. by its diversity it makes it easier to achieve and maintain national unity.
   D. all of the above.

3. The view that the various levels of government are related parts of a single governmental system characterized more by shared functions than by conflict and competition describes which of the following?
   A. Dual federalism
   B. Cooperative federalism
   C. New federalism
   D. Creative federalism

4. The Clean Air Act of 1970, which set federal air quality standards for the whole country but required the states to draft plans to enforce those standards, is an example of _____
   A. dual federalism.
   B. cooperative federalism.
   C. shared federalism.
   D. regulatory federalism.

5. When President Clinton signed the Unfunded Mandates Reform Act into law in March of 1995, it required Congress _____
   A. to help Ohio raise money to comply with the Clean Water Act and the Safe Drinking Water Act.
   B. to help New York City officials modify elevators in subways to accommodate disabled persons.
   C. to enforce regulatory federalism.
   D. to fund requirements placed on the states unless a majority of the House and Senate votes not to do so.

6. Which of the following types of power are exercised by the national government?
   A. Enumerated powers
   B. Implied powers
   C. Inherent powers
   D. All of the above

7. Powers that are held by the federal government and the state governments that are similar but may be exercised independently by each are _____
   A. enumerated powers.
   B. implied powers.
   C. inherent powers.
   D. concurrent powers.

8. The type of power that was granted to the national government by the Supreme Court in the case of *McCulloch v. Maryland* is _____
   A. enumerated.
   B. implied.
   C. inherent.
   D. concurrent.

9. In the case of *United States v. Lopez*, the Supreme Court _____
   A. sharply limited the power of the federal government to intervene in state and local law enforcement.
   B. ruled that the decision restricted the power of Congress, established in the Constitution, to regulate interstate commerce.
   C. ruled 5–4 that Congress had exceeded its authority when it passed a law making it a federal crime to carry a gun within one thousand feet of a school.
   D. all of the above.

10. The supremacy clause of the U.S. Constitution does which of the following?
    A. It makes state constitutions supreme to the U.S. Constitution.
    B. It makes state constitutions and all laws made under them supreme to all laws passed by the U.S. government.
    C. It makes state constitutions and all laws made under them supreme to all treaties entered into by the U.S. government.
    D. None of the above.

11. The clause in the U.S. Constitution that precludes a state from discriminating against a citizen of another state is _____
    A. the privileges and immunities clause.
    B. the full faith and credit clause.
    C. the extradition clause.
    D. the supremacy clause.

12. Which of the following is an example of general purpose grants?
    A. Federal aid to state and local governments that is earmarked for specific purposes such as pollution control, schools, or hospitals
    B. Federal aid to state and local governments that is for general use in a broad area such as community development
    C. Federal aid to state and local governments that may be used by states and localities mostly as they wish
    D. Grants-in-aid

13. The federal form of government established by the 1787 constitution contained all of the provisions EXCEPT _____
    A. distribution of authority between the national government and the states.
    B. delegation of certain powers to the national government.
    C. sharing of some powers between the national government and the states.
    D. establishment of a triumvirate executive branch.

14. The interstate highway system is a partnership between the _____
    A. northern and southern states.
    B. eastern and western states.
    C. national government and the states.
    D. national government and the adjacent countries.

15. Which of the following was NOT one of the indictments against Timothy McVeigh and Terry Nichols for the Oklahoma City bombing?
    A. Using a weapon of mass destruction to kill people and destroy federal property
    B. Using a weapon of mass destruction that caused death and injury
    C. Murdering eight federal law enforcement officers
    D. Creating a riotous condition on federal property

16. Education is a matter that is left primarily to the _____
    A. local governments.
    B. state governments.
    C. national government.
    D. Interstate Council.

ESSAY/PROBLEM QUESTIONS

17. Identify and evaluate the advantages and disadvantages of the federal system in the United States. Evaluate whether the federal system will be able to adapt to the requirements of the next century or whether a unitary system might more effectively adapt.

18. Identify and distinguish between dual federalism, cooperative federalism, creative federalism, new federalism, and regulatory federalism. Evaluate which type of federalism is most appropriate for governing the United States.

19. Explain the pros and cons of federalism in dealing with transportation. When should the national government determine the law and when should the state government determine the law?

20. Describe how our system of federalism worked after the bombing of the Alfred P. Murrah Building.

ANSWER KEY

The following provides the answers and references for the Practice Test questions. Objectives are referenced using the following abbreviations:

T=Textbook Objectives   V=Video Objectives

1. A .... T1 .... Cummings, p. 60
2. A .... T2 .... Cummings, pp. 61–62
3. B .... T3 .... Cummings, p. 65
4. D .... T3 .... Cummings, p. 66
5. D .... T4 .... Cummings, p. 67
6. D .... T5 .... Cummings, p. 68
7. D .... T5 .... Cummings, p. 68
8. B .... T6 .... Cummings, pp. 68–69
9. D .... T6 .... Cummings, p. 71
10. D .... T7 .... Cummings, p. 72
11. A .... T7 .... Cummings, p. 73
12. C .... T8 .... Cummings, p. 79
13. D .... V10 .... Video
14. C .... V11 .... Video
15. D .... V12 .... Video
16. B .... V13 .... Video
17. .... T1, T2, T9 .... Cummings, pp. 59–63, p. 83
18. .... T3 .... Cummings, pp. 65–67
19. .... V11 .... Video
20. .... V12 .... Video

Lesson 5

Intergovernmental Relations

LESSON ASSIGNMENTS

Review the following assignments in order to schedule your time appropriately. Pay careful attention. The titles and numbers of the textbook chapter, the telecourse guide lesson, and the video program may be different from one another.

Text:
> Cummings and Wise, *Democracy Under Pressure*, Chapter 18, "Promoting the General Welfare," pp. 603–606 and pp. 619–622, and Chapter 19, "State and Local Government," pp. 656–667 ("Cities and Suburbs: The Metropolitan Dilemma") and pp. 668–669 ("Intergovernmental Relations" through "The American Challenge").

Video:
> "Intergovernmental Relations" from the series *Voices in Democracy: United States Government*.

Activities:
> One or more activities may be assigned to this lesson. Refer to your syllabus.

OVERVIEW

This lesson examines the contemporary problems facing U.S. cities, where most people live. A crucial component of the problem is the changing demographics of the cities and the suburbs, which has led to both a conflictual and interdependent relationship. We examine the key problems facing inner cities, especially the issues of welfare, public housing, and transportation needs. Previous and ongoing attempts to solve these problems are discussed. This information should help you evaluate whether U.S. political institutions are capable of dealing with the demands of a highly urbanized society.

A focus on the implementation of the Welfare Reform Act demonstrates the complicated but necessary intergovernmental relations between national, state, and local governments. Because the U.S. welfare reform allows for a great deal of creativity, we examine the roles of the different levels of government in Florida and Wisconsin.

LESSON GOAL

You should be able to discuss the intergovernmental relations necessary in solving problems which cross government jurisdictions.

TEXTBOOK OBJECTIVES

The following objectives are designed to help you get the most from the text. Review them before reading the assignment. You may want to write notes to reinforce what you have learned.

1. Describe the conflicting but interdependent relationship between suburbs and cities as they attempt to solve national problems at the local level.

2. Identify the intergovernmental problems in the attempts to revitalize cities, particularly the creation of enterprise zones.

3. Identify recent population trends and their impact on the relationship between national, state, and local governments in regard to problems that involve cities and suburbs.

4. Evaluate urban housing problems and the various attempts to ameliorate the problems.

5. Evaluate urban transportation problems and the various attempts to ameliorate the problems. Discuss the dominance of the interstate highway system.

6. Evaluate whether U.S. political institutions are capable of dealing with the demands of a highly urbanized society.

VIDEO OBJECTIVES

The following objectives are designed to help you get the most from the video segment of this lesson. Review them before watching the video. You may want to write notes to reinforce what you have learned.

7. Identify the intergovernmental activities necessary to carry out the U.S. Welfare Reform Act and discuss the problems that the reforms may bring.

8. Describe the national, state, and local efforts to solve the problems of welfare-to-work in Wisconsin.

9. Describe the national, state, and local efforts to solve the problem of welfare-to-work in Florida.

10. Discuss the future of welfare reform in the United States.

PRACTICE TEST

After reading the assignment, watching the video, and addressing the objectives, you should be able to complete the following Practice Test. Some essay questions in this Practice Test may be included in your exams. When you have completed the Practice Test, turn to the Answer Key to score your answers.

MULTIPLE CHOICE

Select the single best answer. If more than one answer is required, it will be so indicated.

1. Which of the following statements most accurately describes the relationship between the suburbs and cities?
   A. Conflict between the cities and suburbs has lessened due to increased interdependence of the cities and suburbs.
   B. Conflict between the cities and suburbs has increased because the suburban areas do not have to deal with issues such as crime and traffic.
   C. Since urban legislators outnumber suburban ones, they have been able to push through aid to central cities that suburban legislators did not want.
   D. Urban legislators have joined forces with rural legislators to challenge suburban interests.

2. An enterprise zone is _____
   A. an attempt to encourage economic development in poor rural areas.
   B. an attempt to encourage suburban economic development.
   C. an attempt to revitalize inner cities.
   D. an attempt to revitalize inner cities that President Bush supported in a 1992 bill.

3. Public housing programs in the United States have _____
   A. cost billions of dollars, but have been worth it since they generally met the need for better housing.
   B. been plagued by problems such as vandals and high crime rates.
   C. often conflicted with urban renewal program goals.
   D. both B and C.

4. Which of the following correctly describes presidential policy on public housing?
   A. President Kennedy's policy called for the creation of model cities in 150 communities.
   B. The goal of President Reagan's policy was to end construction of low-income housing.
   C. The goal of President Nixon's policy was to end rent subsidies for poor persons.
   D. All of the above.

5. The federal government's interstate highway program _____
   A. pays only a small portion of the cost of the interstate highway program; most of the cost is borne by the states.
   B. has been affected by powerful interest groups with major stakes in highway politics.
   C. has not encouraged development of rapid rail, subway, or bus commuter lines.
   D. is financed strictly from income taxes.

6. According to Don Winstead, there's a wide variety of people on welfare, and that is why _____
   A. there needs to be strict adherence to the regulations.
   B. a community-based solution will be a better solution.
   C. administrators need to be trained in sociological needs.
   D. the costs need to be carefully monitored.

7. The relationships between the federal government, the state government, and the local governments are called _____
   A. governmental corporations.
   B. governmental interactions.
   C. federal relations.
   D. intergovernmental relations.

8. Antonio Riley believes that the old welfare program (AFDC) _____
   A. broke up families.
   B. did not reflect our values.
   C. made people work too hard.
   D. both A and B.

9. One of the strengths of Florida's welfare-to-work program is the _____
   A. partnership between the federal and local governments.
   B. public-private partnership.
   C. number of eligible recipients.
   D. number of job opportunities.

10. Welfare reform is a complex proposition because of _____
    A. interagency rivalry and jealousy.
    B. the controversy over states rights.
    C. fragmented and decentralized governmental jurisdictions.
    D. systematized and unresponsive employment standards.

ESSAY/PROBLEM QUESTIONS

11. Identify recent population trends and describe their impact on the relationship between cities and suburbs. Be sure to discuss both the conflict and interdependence in this relationship.

12. Describe the problem of transportation in the cities. Discuss past efforts to deal with the problem, particularly addressing the issue of dominance by the highway systems and efforts to bring mass transit to cities. How do these transportation problems relate to other problems that plague the cities? What roles do state and national governments play in the transportation problems?

13. Describe the problem of housing in inner cities. Discuss past efforts to deal with this problem and evaluate whether U.S. institutions are capable of dealing with this problem. Do you think that the government is responsible for solving this problem?

14. Describe the pros and cons of welfare reform in Wisconsin and how the national, state, and local governments are involved.

15. Compare the welfare-to-work reforms in Wisconsin and Florida. What are the positive and negative points of each state's plan?

16. After examining and analyzing welfare reform in Florida and Wisconsin, describe the best way to ensure that people can work and not be dependent on government. What will happen with your plan if there is large scale unemployment in some future years?

ANSWER KEY

The following provides the answers and references for the Practice Test questions. Objectives are referenced using the following abbreviations:

T=Textbook Objectives   V=Video Objectives

1.	A	T1, T3	Cummings, pp. 656–657
2.	C	T2	Cummings, p. 658
3.	D	T4	Cummings, pp. 660–661
4.	C	T4	Cummings, p. 661
5.	B	T5	Cummings, pp. 662–663
6.	B	V7	Video
7.	D	V7	Video
8.	D	V8	Video
9.	B	V9	Video
10.	C	V10	Video
11.		T1, T3	Cummings, pp. 656–667
12.		T2, T5	Cummings, pp. 662–663
13.		T4, T6	Cummings, pp. 659–662
14.		V9	Video
15.		V10	Video
16.		V7, V8, V9, V10	Video

Lesson 5—Intergovernmental Relations

Lesson 6

Public Opinion and Political Socialization

LESSON ASSIGNMENTS

Review the following assignments in order to schedule your time appropriately. Pay careful attention. The titles and numbers of the textbook chapter, the telecourse guide lesson, and the video program may be different from one another.

Text:
> Cummings and Wise, *Democracy Under Pressure*, Chapter 6, "Public Opinion," pp. 169–191.

Video:
> "Public Opinion and Political Socialization" from the series *Voices in Democracy: United States Government*.

Activities:
> One or more activities may be assigned to this lesson. Refer to your syllabus.

OVERVIEW

This lesson examines the topic of public opinion and explores its impact on public policy. We examine how political views are formed through the process of political socialization, particularly looking at the role of the family, religion, schools, and the media. Group influences on public opinion are also explored. We examine the process of measuring and reporting public opinion and evaluate the impact that such polling may have on public policy. This lesson also seeks to explain how political socialization occurs throughout life and how that background affects people's perceptions of political events.

LESSON GOAL

Identify the factors that influence political socialization and explain the formation of issue positions based on political socialization.

TEXTBOOK OBJECTIVES

The following objectives are designed to help you get the most from the text. Review them before reading the assignment. You may want to write notes to reinforce what you have learned.

1. Define and distinguish between *public opinion*, *special publics*, and *political opinion*.

2. Explain how people form their political views, and discuss the role of family, education, religion, gender, ethnicity, region, and the media in the formation of political views.

3. Discuss group influence on public opinion. Be able to define *reference groups*, *primary groups*, and *secondary groups*.

4. Identify and explain the qualities of public opinion. Be conversant with the basic language of opinion polling including terms such as *population* or *universe, random samples, quota sampling, cluster sampling*, and *exit polling*. Understand why and how polls can be wrong. Understand the impact that polls may have on politics.

5. Identify the generalities concerning beliefs among people in the United States.

6. Examine the factors that explain political participation.

7. Discuss the role of public opinion in national policymaking, especially given the qualities of public opinion in the United States.

VIDEO OBJECTIVES

The following objectives are designed to help you get the most from the video segment of this lesson. Review them before watching the video. You may want to write notes to reinforce what you have learned.

8. Explain the factors that influence political socialization.

9. Examine the major political socialization influences on young children and adolescents.

10. Examine the major political socialization influences on adults.

11. Explain the formation of issue positions based on political socialization, focusing on black and white reactions to the O. J. Simpson verdict.

PRACTICE TEST

After reading the assignment, watching the video, and addressing the objectives, you should be able to complete the following Practice Test. Some essay questions in this Practice Test may be included in your exams. When you have completed the Practice Test, turn to the Answer Key to score your answers.

MULTIPLE CHOICE

Select the single best answer. If more than one answer is required, it will be so indicated.

1. "The expression of attitudes about government and politics" is the definition of which of the following?
   A. Political socialization
   B. Public opinion
   C. Quota sampling
   D. Interest groups

2. Which of the following is the definition of *political socialization*?
   A. The expression of attitudes about government and politics
   B. An opinion about music, movies, or fashions
   C. The process by which a person acquires a set of political attitudes and forms opinions about social issues
   D. All of the above

3. According to Robert E. Lane, which of the following "incubates" political attitudes and opinions?
   A. Elementary schools
   B. Professional groups
   C. Churches
   D. Families

4. Which of the following would be classified as a secondary reference group?
   A. Friends
   B. Family
   C. Labor unions
   D. All of the above

5. Which of the following qualities measures whether or not a person has a mild opinion or a deeply felt opinion on a subject?
   A. Direction
   B. Intensity
   C. Stability
   D. All of the above

6. The mechanism that is used to measure and analyze the qualities of public opinion is _____
   A. political socialization.
   B. a political poll.
   C. political participation.
   D. none of the above.

7. Which of the following statements is true regarding political polls?
   A. Political polls always accurately predict the outcome of an election.
   B. Political polls measure opinion only at the moment the survey is taken.
   C. Quota sampling has a lower margin of error than has a random sample.
   D. All of the above.

8. Which of the following is correct concerning the political beliefs of Americans?
   A. Americans seem to be pragmatic, approaching each issue as it comes up and judging it on its merits.
   B. Americans have a fixed, coherent set of political beliefs.
   C. Americans do not have clear preferences on specific issues, but often their convictions are interrelated.
   D. All of the above.

9. In your authors' opinion, which of the following is a correct statement concerning the American voter?
   A. Voters have begun to evaluate candidates and parties more in terms of their party affiliation than in terms of their issue positions.
   B. Political participation as measured by voting is low, especially in nonpresidential elections.
   C. Americans are very well informed about government and many public issues.
   D. All of the above.

10. Which of the following statements is true about the public knowledge of Americans, according to surveys conducted in 2000?
    A. Only 4 percent of Americans knew the name of the speaker of the U.S. House of Representatives.
    B. Only half of those questioned knew that there were one hundred senators.
    C. Four in ten Americans did not know who was the vice president of the United States.
    D. All of the above.

11. The single most important factor in political socialization seems to be _____
    A. family.
    B. ethnicity.
    C. gender.
    D. education.

12. Children tend to identify with the same political party as their _____
    A. parents.
    B. grandparents.
    C. teachers.
    D. siblings.

13. Students may begin to move away from their parents' behaviors, beliefs, and political identifications by _____
    A. elementary school.
    B. middle school.
    C. high school.
    D. college.

14. The preamble of the United Auto Workers union constitution interested and influenced a young Pancho Medrano because it _____
    A. offered handsome salaries.
    B. provided excellent benefits.
    C. allowed no discrimination against anybody.
    D. guaranteed a job to all who wanted to work hard.

15. Mago became a citizen of the United States so that he _____
    A. would not have to worry about being deported.
    B. could find a better paying job.
    C. would be eligible for college scholarships.
    D. would have the right to vote.

16. According to Professor Jewelle Taylor Gibbs, there is a tremendous legacy of mistrust, anger, and alienation toward the _____
    A. schools and the entire educational system.
    B. doctors and all health care systems.
    C. entire mass media industry.
    D. police and criminal justice system.

ESSAY/PROBLEM QUESTIONS

17. Identify and explain three qualities of public opinion. Give an example of a question that would measure each of these qualities.

18. Define *political socialization*. Identify the main agents of political socialization. Identify which of these are primary agents and which are secondary agents, and explain the effect each of these agents has on the process.

19. Evaluate the impact of polls on public policy and elections. Do they serve a valid purpose in democratic governance?

20. Remembering your young childhood, describe experiences in which you believe you were politically socialized. Are your experiences typical of those described in the video program?

21. Relate the major political socialization influences of your young adulthood. How do they compare with those of Pancho Medrano, Abigail Wright, or A. K. Mago?

22. According to Professor Jewelle Taylor Gibbs, why would African Americans be likely to view the verdict in the O. J. Simpson murder trial differently than European Americans?

ANSWER KEY

The following provides the answers and references for the Practice Test questions. Objectives are referenced using the following abbreviations:

T=Textbook Objectives   V=Video Objectives

#	Ans	Obj	Reference
1.	B	T1	Cummings, p. 170
2.	C	T2	Cummings, p. 171
3.	D	T2	Cummings, p. 172
4.	C	T3	Cummings, p. 176
5.	B	T4	Cummings, p. 178
6.	B	T4	Cummings, p. 178
7.	B	T4	Cummings, p. 181
8.	A	T5	Cummings, p. 183
9.	B	T6	Cummings, p. 184
10.	D	T7	Cummings, p. 184
11.	D	V8	Video
12.	A	V9	Video
13.	C	V9	Video
14.	C	V10	Video
15.	D	V10	Video
16.	D	V11	Video
17.		T4	Cummings, pp. 177–178
18.		T2, T3	Cummings, pp. 171–177
19.		T7	Cummings, pp. 178–182
20.		V9	Video
21.		V10	Video
22.		V11	Video

Lesson 7

Participation in Democracy

LESSON ASSIGNMENTS

Review the following assignments in order to schedule your time appropriately. Pay careful attention. The titles and numbers of the textbook chapter, the telecourse guide lesson, and the video program may be different from one another.

Text:
>Cummings and Wise, *Democracy Under Pressure*, Chapter 11, "Voting Behavior and Elections," pp. 325–337 (through "Rational Choice" only).

Video:
>"Participation in Democracy" from the series *Voices in Democracy: United States Government*.

Activities:
>One or more activities may be assigned to this lesson. Refer to your syllabus.

OVERVIEW

This lesson examines citizen participation in the electoral process, legislative initiative action, and protest movements. Current trends in voting behavior are identified. Specifically, we examine socioeconomic and psychological factors that influence voter turnout and voter preferences. The information discussed will help you to evaluate how voter participation in the United States fits the expectations of democratic governance.

    The legislative initiative action is explored by examining the political action taken to pass Proposition 215 in California. Protest activity requires organization and planning to be effective and to have an influence. The American Indian Movement in Colorado exemplifies the action taken by the people to effectively get their message across. There are many ways to take an active part in your democracy. However, many people do not take part because apathy (a belief that political action is useless) is very high in the United States.

LESSON GOAL

You should be able to explain the wide variety of political participation in our United States democracy and how you might take political action.

TEXTBOOK OBJECTIVES

The following objectives are designed to help you get the most from the text. Review them before reading the assignment. You may want to write notes to reinforce what you have learned.

1. Identify recent trends in voter turnout in the United States.

2. Evaluate the impact of low voter turnout on democratic governance.

3. Identify the socioeconomic factors that affect voter turnout and voter attitudes and preferences.

4. Discuss why such a large portion of the population has become nonvoters. Why do certain voters tend to support political parties?

5. Discuss and evaluate the sociological and psychological factors that influence the individual's voting decisions.

6. Identify and discuss the three sets of psychological factors that affect individual voting decisions. Define and discuss *retrospective voting*.

7. Given the factors that have been shown to influence voting, evaluate the rationality of U.S. voters. Are the decisions they make in the polling booth based on the criteria that democratic principles would require?

VIDEO OBJECTIVES

The following objectives are designed to help you get the most from the video segment of this lesson. Review them before watching the video. You may want to write notes to reinforce what you have learned.

8. Explain the importance of "doing something."

9. Describe the legislative action by citizens called an "initiative."

10. Describe the basic components of a political action movement, such as California's Proposition 215, an initiative that became law in California.

11. Describe the impact a small group can have if it becomes politically active. Use the American Indian Movement's protest of the Columbus Day celebration in Denver as an example.

12. Explain the importance of political participation in a democracy.

PRACTICE TEST

After reading the assignment, watching the video, and addressing the objectives, you should be able to complete the following Practice Test. Some essay questions in this Practice Test may be included in your exams. When you have completed the Practice Test, turn to the Answer Key to score your answers.

MULTIPLE CHOICE

Select the single best answer. If more than one answer is required, it will be so indicated.

1. Which of the following has a higher voter turnout than the United States?
   A. Canada
   B. Great Britain
   C. Germany
   D. All of the above

2. When one studies the effect a person's gender, ethnic background, and education have on how that person votes, one is studying _____
   A. psychological factors.
   B. socioeconomic factors.
   C. occupational factors.
   D. none of the above.

3. Which of the following persons would be the most likely to vote?
   A. A Jewish female with a degree from graduate school
   B. A Protestant white male with a grade school education
   C. A Catholic male with a high school education
   D. An African American female who works on a production line

4. Which of the following persons is the most likely to be a nonvoter in the United States?
   A. A person who is advantageously situated in the social system
   B. A person whose intensity of partisan preference is high
   C. A person who is disadvantageously situated in the social system
   D. A person who has a high sense of civic duty

5. A person whose affiliations are pulling that person in opposite directions is said to be _____
   A. highly partisan.
   B. possessed with a high degree of intensity.
   C. cross-pressured.
   D. possessed with a high degree of civic duty.

6. In presidential elections since 1980, how have men and women differed in the manner in which they voted?
   A. There is no difference.
   B. Men have voted for the Democratic candidate more often than women have.
   C. Women have voted for the Democratic candidate more often than men have.
   D. Women have voted for the Republican candidate more often than men have.

7. Regarding party identification, which of the following is correct?
   A. Republicans outnumber Democrats, but the gap is narrowing.
   B. Although party identification remains a key factor in American politics, there are signs that it may be growing somewhat less important.
   C. There has been a decrease in ticket-splitting in most of the elections since World War II.
   D. All of the above.

8. How do issues affect the manner in which a person votes?
   A. Human beings are not selective in accepting political messages and therefore are not affected by issues.
   B. Certain major issues or issues that affect people directly cause voters to tune in and form definite party preferences.
   C. There have not been any elections in which substantial issue voting occurred.
   D. None of the above.

9. People become politically active when they organize because they _____
   A. have an innate need to join.
   B. share common goals and desires.
   C. want to include community action in their resumes.
   D. can't accomplish anything alone.

10. An initiative is an electoral device by which interested citizens in some states can _____
    A. take politicians out of office.
    B. pass a law outside of the state legislature.
    C. veto legislation passed by Congress.
    D. veto action taken by the president.

11. All of the following were viewed as shortcomings in California's Proposition 215 EXCEPT there was _____
    A. nothing to regulate how potent the marijuana could be.
    B. no provision to determine who would regulate marijuana.
    C. no one to be held responsible for drug interactions.
    D. no way to protect the purchasers from arrest.

12. The major intent of the American Indian Movement in Denver and Pueblo over the Columbus Day celebration was to _____
    A. start educating people.
    B. demand financial retribution.
    C. focus on broken treaties.
    D. embarrass the city fathers of Denver and Pueblo.

13. All of the following are examples of apathy in people in the U.S. system of government EXCEPT _____
    A. they don't believe politicians listen.
    B. they believe they are politically active in their communities.
    C. they don't believe they can make a difference for change.
    D. they don't believe their vote counts.

ESSAY/PROBLEM QUESTIONS

14. Identify three socioeconomic factors that affect the way that a person votes, and discuss the manner in which each factor affects voter turnout and voter preferences.

15. Identify the three main psychological factors that affect individual voting preferences, and discuss the manner in which each factor affects voter preferences. Define *retrospective voting* and explain how it fits within the study of psychological factors.

16. Democratic theory is based on the principle that the mass public will participate in government by voting and making informed choices when they vote. Based on the evidence concerning voter turnout and the factors that influence voter choice, do the citizens in the United States currently meet these standards?

17. List the ways in which people can have an influence on politics in the U.S. democracy. Describe two methods and their successes or failures as exemplified by the video.

18. If you had lived in California when the vote on Proposition 215 was taken, how would you have voted? Why? Explain using arguments from the video.

19. Explain the importance of political participation in a democracy. What are the costs of not participating?

ANSWER KEY

The following provides the answers and references for the Practice Test questions. Objectives are referenced using the following abbreviations:
T=Textbook Objectives   V=Video Objectives

#	Answer	Objective	Reference
1.	D	T1	Cummings, p. 328
2.	B	T2	Cummings, pp. 327–328
3.	A	T2	Cummings, pp. 328–329
4.	C	T3	Cummings, p. 330
5.	C	T4	Cummings, p. 331
6.	C	T4	Cummings, pp. 333–334
7.	B	T5	Cummings, pp. 334–335
8.	B	T5	Cummings, p. 336
9.	B	V8	Video
10.	B	V9	Video
11.	D	V10	Video
12.	A	V11	Video
13.	B	V12	Video
14.		T2, T3, T5	Cummings, pp. 331–334
15.		T5, T6	Cummings, pp. 334–337
16.		T5, T6, T7	Cummings, pp. 327–337
17.		V8, V10, V11	Video
18.		V10	Video
19.		V12	Video

Lesson 8

Mass Media and Government

LESSON ASSIGNMENTS

Review the following assignments in order to schedule your time appropriately. Pay careful attention. The titles and numbers of the textbook chapter, the telecourse guide lesson, and the video program may be different from one another.

Text:
> Cummings and Wise, *Democracy Under Pressure*, Chapter 8, "The Media and Politics," pp. 215–222 and pp. 225–245.

Video:
> "Mass Media and Government" from the series *Voices in Democracy: United States Government*.

Activities:
> One or more activities may be assigned to this lesson. Refer to your syllabus.

OVERVIEW

This lesson examines the role of the media in politics. The special constitutional protections which the press has received are examined. Particularly, the lesson traces the Supreme Court's rulings on prior restraint and libel. We also examine the tension between freedom of press and other societal concerns such as national security, fair trials, and criminal justice. We also evaluate the symbiotic and adversarial relationship between the press and government. And finally, we examine the accusations that the media are biased and that the government manipulates the press.

LESSON GOAL

You should be able to discuss the interdependent relationship between media and government in the U.S. democracy and explain the responsibility of the reader/viewer in discerning the truth.

TEXTBOOK OBJECTIVES

The following objectives are designed to help you get the most from the text. Review them before reading the assignment. You may want to write notes to reinforce what you have learned.

1. Explain why the Constitution and the courts have given special protections to the press.

2. Describe the evolution of the U.S. media from print to television media and evaluate the impact that each has had on elections, voters, and political leadership.

3. Describe the protection against prior restraint. Discuss the *New York Times,* the *Progressive,* and the CNN cases, in light of prior restraint. Examine the tension between the right of public access to information and the need for national security.

4. Examine the tension between freedom of the press and the constitutional guarantee of a fair trial. Evaluate recent cases that highlighted this issue, particularly in regard to pretrial publicity and cameras in the courts.

5. Examine the tension between freedom of the press and confidentiality for news reporters and their sources. Evaluate the cases of Earl Caldwell and Myron Farber in regard to this tension. Describe the current status of shield laws.

6. Describe libel in the context of freedom of the press, particularly the *New York Times* rule. Examine the concept of a public figure and how this concept has evolved through Supreme Court decisions over the last thirty-five years.

7. Describe the symbiotic and adversarial relationship between the press and the government.

8. Examine the debates concerning media bias and government manipulation of information and the press, particularly in foreign policy events.

VIDEO OBJECTIVES

The following objectives are designed to help you get the most from the video segment of this lesson. Review them before watching the video. You may want to write notes to reinforce what you have learned.

9. Discuss the role of a free press in the U.S. democracy.

10. Describe the changes in how the media cover wartime activities, and discuss how government and media have manipulated war news.

11. Discuss the important relationship between the press and the president, including citing the use of trial balloons, spins, and backgrounders.

12. Explain the responsibility of the reader/viewer in discerning the truth.

PRACTICE TEST

After reading the assignment, watching the video, and addressing the objectives, you should be able to complete the following Practice Test. Some essay questions in this Practice Test may be included in your exams. When you have completed the Practice Test, turn to the Answer Key to score your answers.

MULTIPLE CHOICE

Select the single best answer. If more than one answer is required, it will be so indicated.

1. Which of the following is true about freedom of the press?
    A. It was included in the original draft of the Constitution.
    B. It was added as an amendment to the Constitution in the 1900s.
    C. It is an inherent freedom not explicitly given in the Constitution.
    D. It was passed as part of the Bill of Rights freedoms.

2. Which of the following presidents held the first live, televised presidential news conference?
   A. Harry Truman
   B. Dwight Eisenhower
   C. John F. Kennedy
   D. Richard M. Nixon

3. Which of the following factors has contributed to the shrinking of the newspaper industry since the 1980s?
   A. The advent of CNN and cable television
   B. The movement of Americans from the cities to the suburbs after World War II
   C. Newspapers have become too boring
   D. Both A and B

4. Under the First Amendment protection of freedom of the press, the Court has ruled that _____
   A. the government's determination of what constitutes national security will not always outweigh a newspaper's right to publish.
   B. the prohibition against prior restraint of the press does not apply to any case that involves national security interests.
   C. states may exercise prior restraint when there is a compelling state interest.
   D. the government could prohibit the publication of a series based on the secret history of the Vietnam War since it threatened national security.

5. Which is true of television in the courtroom?
   A. It is constitutional.
   B. As of 1996, forty-seven states allow cameras in the courtroom.
   C. Judges can exercise their discretion to bar television.
   D. All of the above.

6. When deciding the *Richmond Newspapers, Inc. v. Virginia* case, the Supreme Court ruled that _____
   A. the press could be barred from the courtroom if the defendant waived the right of an open trial.
   B. trials must be open to the public and the press except in the most unusual cases.
   C. television cameras must be barred from court proceedings.
   D. gag rules are not a violation of the First Amendment guarantees of freedom of the press.

7. In the *Caldwell* case the Supreme Court ruled that _____
   A. reporters have the constitutional right to protect their sources.
   B. reporters do not have the constitutional right to protect their sources.
   C. gag rules do not violate the First Amendment's guarantees of freedom of the press.
   D. television cameras may be constitutionally barred from the courtroom.

8. Which of the following is a true statement?
   A. Truth has always been an absolute defense in libel cases.
   B. The Supreme Court has made it almost impossible to libel a public official unless the statement has been made with "actual malice."
   C. A person who accepts public funding for research does not become a "public figure" and therefore has the same protections against personal attacks as a private person.
   D. All of the above.

9. Which of the following is an accurate description of the relationship between the press and government?
   A. They are like heavyweight boxers circling each other warily in the ring.
   B. They are adversaries who need each other.
   C. They are mutually dependent.
   D. All of the above.

10. When a government official or employee divulges information to an individual reporter on the condition that the official remain anonymous, this is known as _____
    A. a symbol.
    B. a backgrounder.
    C. a leak.
    D. a manipulation.

11. Which of the following statements about the press is true?
    A. The public has a low level of confidence in it.
    B. Several correspondents in Washington have become media "stars" who appear on weekly political talk shows and command huge speaking fees from the very industries and groups they may cover.
    C. Some journalists are open to charges of conflict of interest.
    D. All of the above.

12. Which of the following statements accurately describes the press during the Gulf War?
    A. The press was confined to pools whose movements and access were restricted.
    B. The Secretary of State bragged about outwitting the press during the war.
    C. The treatment of the press led to new rules being drawn up that would allow more open and independent reporting in future wars.
    D. All of the above.

13. The first president to effectively use television was _____
    A. Franklin Roosevelt.
    B. Dwight Eisenhower.
    C. John Kennedy.
    D. Richard Nixon.

14. The mass media found covering the Gulf War very frustrating because of the way _____
    A. the public reacted to the news.
    B. the military conducted the operation.
    C. the Pentagon managed the news.
    D. Congress appropriated funds for media coverage.

15. One way the president personally attempts to persuade Congress and the American people to support the administration's agenda is to _____
    A. recruit Cabinet members from Congress.
    B. send his staff to the people.
    C. hold news conferences.
    D. hold special dinners at the White House.

16. A fact or theory that is given to a reporter to print in order to determine its popularity is called a _____
    A. trial balloon.
    B. spin.
    C. backgrounder.
    D. all of the above.

17. A free press provides an independent _____
    A. source of research for the lobbyists.
    B. check on the people and institutions of government.
    C. contributor to developing public policy.
    D. interpreter of judicial policy.

ESSAY/PROBLEM QUESTIONS

18. Examine whether the press is objective. You should discuss the accusations that the press is biased and discuss how the relationship between the press and the government might affect objectivity.

19. Define *prior restraint* and *libel*. How do these concepts relate to freedom of press? Discuss and evaluate how the Supreme Court has protected or curbed freedom of press.

20. Discuss the several levels of tension that exist between freedom of press and other societal concerns, such as fair trials, terrorism, and criminal justice.

21. Explain the role that the media play during wartime. Do you think this role has been abused? Why/Why not?

22. Does the public need to know all about the personal lives of public officials, especially the president? Why/Why not?

23. What is the role of the press secretary? According to Marlin Fitzwater, why is it a difficult job?

ANSWER KEY

The following provides the answers and references for the Practice Test questions. Objectives are referenced using the following abbreviations:
T=Textbook Objectives   V=Video Objectives

1.	D	T1	Cummings, p. 216
2.	C	T2	Cummings, p. 217
3.	D	T2	Cummings, pp. 220–221
4.	A	T3	Cummings, pp. 225–226
5.	D	T4	Cummings, pp. 227–228
6.	B	T4	Cummings, p. 228
7.	B	T5	Cummings, pp. 228–229
8.	D	T6	Cummings, pp. 229–230
9.	D	T7, V11	Cummings, p. 232
10.	C	T7, V11	Cummings, p. 232
11.	D	T8, V12	Cummings, p. 237
12.	D	T8	Cummings, p. 242
13.	C	V9	Video
14.	C	V10	Video
15.	C	V11	Video
16.	A	V11	Video
17.	B	V12	Video
18.		T2, T8	Cummings, pp. 232–242
19.		T3, T6	Cummings, pp. 225–231
20.		T4, T5	Cummings, pp. 227–232
21.		V10	Video
22.		V11	Video
23.		V11	Video

Lesson 8—Mass Media and Government

Lesson 9

Interest Groups

LESSON ASSIGNMENTS

Review the following assignments in order to schedule your time appropriately. Pay careful attention. The titles and numbers of the textbook chapter, the telecourse guide lesson, and the video program may be different from one another.

Text:
> Cummings and Wise, *Democracy Under Pressure*, Chapter 7, "Interest Groups," pp. 193–213.

Video:
> "Interest Groups" from the series *Voices in Democracy: United States Government*.

Activities:
> One or more activities may be assigned to this lesson. Refer to your syllabus.

OVERVIEW

This lesson examines the different types of interest groups and the role they play in our democratic society. Interest groups are examined in the context of the pluralist theory of democracy. Specifically we examine who participates in interest groups and which interest groups are involved in politics. We examine how interest groups operate and we critique their strategies and their ability to impact public policy. This section also looks specifically at the influence of political action committees (PACs) on elections and public policy and evaluates recent attempts to reform their influence on campaigns. This section will provide you with information necessary to evaluate how participation in interest groups and interest group influence should fit within the broad framework of democracy.

Interest groups also combine to form strong coalitions to stop or to pass legislation and to influence government decisions and even judicial action. Sometimes public interest groups are involved in trying to reform political action money, which influences elections.

LESSON GOAL

Identify the major types of interest groups, describe how they function, illustrate their techniques for influencing the branches of government, and explain the pros and cons of campaign finance reform.

TEXTBOOK OBJECTIVES

The following objectives are designed to help you get the most from the text. Review them before reading the assignment. You may want to write notes to reinforce what you have learned.

1. Explain and critique elite theory of democracy.

2. Explain and critique pluralist theory of democracy.

3. Define *interest groups* and identify what groups tend to belong to interest groups and what groups tend not to belong.

4. Explain how interest groups operate. Identify and critique their strategies.

5. Define and identify examples of *public interest groups* and *single-issue interest groups*.

6. Define and identify examples of *political action committees* (PACs). Evaluate their strategies for influencing public policy.

7. Discuss recent attempts to regulate interest groups and evaluate the hurdles in trying to implement reform.

8. Evaluate the impact of interest groups on policymaking and elections, particularly the impact of PACs, in light of the assumptions of pluralist democracy.

VIDEO OBJECTIVES

The following objectives are designed to help you get the most from the video segment of this lesson. Review them before watching the video. You may want to write notes to reinforce what you have learned.

9. List and describe the major types of interest groups.

10. Define *interest groups* and describe how they function.

11. Illustrate some of the techniques used by interest groups to influence the three branches of government.

12. List and explain some of the pros and cons of interest group reform (political action committee money.)

PRACTICE TEST

After reading the assignment, watching the video, and addressing the objectives, you should be able to complete the following Practice Test. Some essay questions in this Practice Test may be included in your exams. When you have completed the Practice Test, turn to the Answer Key to score your answers.

MULTIPLE CHOICE

Select the single best answer. If more than one answer is required, it will be so indicated.

1. Elitist theory argues that _____
   A. many conflicting groups within the community have access to government officials and compete with one another in an effort to influence policy decisions.
   B. "the people" govern through political leaders who are nominated as candidates of political parties or who run as independents and are elected by the voters.
   C. powerful people prevent certain issues from ever reaching the public arena as they control the agenda, thus determining which public policy questions will be debated or even considered.
   D. none of the above.

2. Which of the following, according to your authors, is a correct assessment of pluralism?
   A. It meets the criteria to qualify as a democratic system according to the classic democratic model.
   B. It represents individuals in an equal manner.
   C. It consists of competing groups of elite and therefore falls far short of the classic democratic model.
   D. It provides a means whereby the powerless, the poor, and the consumer have a way to compete in a society.

3. A private group who attempts to influence the government to respond to the shared attitudes of its members is _____
   A. an interest group.
   B. a political party.
   C. an agent of socialization.
   D. an elitist system.

4. Which of the following statements accurately describes interest groups in the United States?
   A. There are relatively few groups in the United States compared to other countries.
   B. Approximately one-third of the population does not belong to an organized group.
   C. Nearly half of those who belong to groups belong to groups that have little relation to politics.
   D. Both B and C.

5. Communication with legislators and other government officials to try to influence their decisions is _____
   A. lobbying.
   B. political socialization.
   C. political polling.
   D. none of the above.

6. Which of the following branches of government do lobbyists attempt to influence?
   A. The legislative
   B. The executive
   C. The judicial (courts)
   D. All of the above

7. A citizen writing or telephoning a member of Congress to express their viewpoint on a policy issue is an example of _____
   A. lobbying.
   B. grass-roots pressure.
   C. mass publicity.
   D. political socialization.

8. Which of the following public interest groups is among the Ralph Nader network?
   A. Public Citizen
   B. The Health Research Group
   C. The Center for Study of Responsive Law
   D. All of the above

9. What are organizations that are sometimes independent but that more often are the political arms of corporations, labor unions, or interest groups and are established to contribute to candidates or to work for general political goals?
   A. Political socialization
   B. Political action committees (PACs)
   C. Lobbying
   D. Political parties

10. Which of the following powerful organizations contributed the most money to candidates in the 1998 congressional campaigns?
    A. Committee on Political Education (COPE)
    B. Common Cause
    C. Realtors Political Action Committee
    D. Congress Watch

11. Which of the following has led to the rise of political action committees (PACs)?
    A. The decline in the power of political parties has forced candidates to turn to interest groups for money.
    B. The publicity given to PACs in recent years has encouraged the formation of even more such committees.
    C. Changes in the structure of Congress has reduced the power of committee chairs; as a result, power has become fragmented among many subcommittees, each of which is cultivated by various lobbyists.
    D. All of the above.

12. Which of the following benefit the most from interest group politics?
    A. Minorities
    B. Consumers
    C. Poorly educated people from the lower economic class
    D. Business and manufacturing interests

13. All of the following are major types of interest groups EXCEPT _____
    A. single-issue.
    B. public (broad based).
    C. business or labor.
    D. liberal or conservative.

14. Which of the following is NOT a function of interest groups?
    A. They provide a vehicle for grass-roots political participation.
    B. They channel information on key issues to the general public.
    C. They serve as buffers between the president and Congress.
    D. They monitor the performance of federal officials and programs.

15. Partnering with the National Rifle Association to fight the passage of the terrorism bill, the American Civil Liberties Union used the media in all of the following ways EXCEPT to _____
    A. provide fascinating stories about the coalition's efforts to defeat the bill.
    B. develop an effective public information campaign promoting the coalition's position.
    C. brief them about the elements of the bill.
    D. expose the collaboration of the coalition as a conspiracy.

16. According to Senator Mitch McConnell, the most important reform which protects the right of individuals, groups, candidates, and parties to speak to the citizens of the United States without government interference is the _____
    A. Declaration of Independence.
    B. First Amendment.
    C. Civil Rights Act of 1964.
    D. Voting Rights Act of 1965.

ESSAY/PROBLEM QUESTIONS

17. Describe and evaluate the role of U.S. interest groups in our democracy. You will want to be sure to include an analysis of who does or does not participate in interest groups and whether the groups have political goals. You will also want to include an analysis of interest group impact on elections and public policymaking.

18. Define the term *interest groups*. Identify the main strategies used by these groups and give examples. Which branches of the government are subjected to these activities? How legitimate are these activities in a democratic society, compared to other forms of participation such as voting?

19. Define what is meant by a *political action committee* (PAC). Identify and comment on the goals of two such committees. How or why did the U.S. Supreme Court's decision in *Buckley v. Valeo* have such an important impact on the formation of PACs? Discuss who benefits the most from PAC activities and explain why they benefit from PAC activities.

20. Using the Sierra Club and American Civil Liberties Union as examples, elaborate on the basic techniques that many interest groups use to influence the three branches of government.

21. List some of the arguments for and against campaign finance reform. Explain the possible effects these reforms might have on the political process in the United States.

ANSWER KEY

The following provides the answers and references for the Practice Test questions. Objectives are referenced using the following abbreviations:

T=Textbook Objectives   V=Video Objectives

#	Ans	Obj	Reference
1.	C	T1	Cummings, p. 194
2.	C	T2	Cummings, p. 195
3.	A	T3	Cummings, p. 195
4.	D	T3	Cummings, p. 196
5.	A	T4	Cummings, p. 197
6.	D	T4	Cummings, p. 197
7.	B	T4, V11	Cummings, p. 201, Video
8.	D	T5	Cummings, pp. 203–205
9.	B	T6, V12	Cummings, p. 206, Video
10.	C	T6, T8	Cummings, p. 207
11.	D	T6, T7	Cummings, p. 206
12.	D	T8	Cummings, p. 210
13.	D	V9	Video
14.	C	V10	Video
15.	D	V11	Video
16.	B	V12	Video
17.		T2, T3, T8	Cummings, pp. 193–210
18.		T3, T4, V11	Cummings, pp. 193–202, Video
19.		T6, T7, V12	Cummings, pp. 206–208, Video
20.		V11	Video
21.		V12	Video

Lesson 10

Political Parties

LESSON ASSIGNMENTS

Review the following assignments in order to schedule your time appropriately. Pay careful attention. The titles and numbers of the textbook chapter, the telecourse guide lesson, and the video program may be different from one another.

Text:
> Cummings and Wise, *Democracy Under Pressure*, Chapter 9, "Political Parties," pp. 247–279.

Video:
> "Political Parties" from the series *Voices in Democracy: United States Government*.

Activities:
> One or more activities may be assigned to this lesson. Refer to your syllabus.

OVERVIEW

This lesson examines the role of political parties in U.S. politics. It explores the function of political parties in our system of government and examines the historical development of political parties. We also explain why our competitive two-party system survives, while minor third parties continually fail to compete fully with the two major parties. This lesson also distinguishes between the philosophies and issue positions of the Democratic and Republican parties and describes the typical identifier of each party. Several recent changes relating to political parties and their role in politics are explored: the decline in party identification and the declining role of national conventions in the presidential selection process. Ultimately, this lesson should enable you to evaluate the proper role of political parties in a democratic society and to evaluate what the future may hold for political parties in the United States.

LESSON GOAL

Describe the primary responsibilities of political parties at all levels, how individuals can get involved in party activities, and the role of third parties.

TEXTBOOK OBJECTIVES

The following objectives are designed to help you get the most from the text. Review them before reading the assignment. You may want to write notes to reinforce what you have learned.

1. Define *political parties* and explain the functions that they perform.

2. Explain the impact of the historical roots of our present political parties and explain the differences in their regional and philosophical roots.

3. Explain why we have a competitive two-party system and why third parties have not been able to successfully compete with the two major parties.

4. Explain why political party identification has waned and why political parties perceive that some of their role in politics is being taken over by other institutions.

5. Examine the commonly accepted descriptions of party identifiers for the Democratic and Republican parties. Describe the two parties' philosophies towards government and their positions on major policy issues.

6. Identify some of the minor parties using Key's classification of doctrinal and transient parties.

7. Describe the implications of decentralization in party organization on building majorities for election, policy positions, and governance.

8. Explain the changing role of the party national conventions in the presidential selection process and evaluate how the primary and caucus systems have eclipsed the great national sideshow.

9. Discuss whether political parties, which were not mentioned in the Constitution, can avoid being accountable to the public in ways that elected officials cannot avoid.

10. Evaluate the role of parties in the future.

VIDEO OBJECTIVES

The following objectives are designed to help you get the most from the video segment of this lesson. Review them before watching the video. You may want to write notes to reinforce what you have learned.

11. Describe the primary responsibilities of political parties at the local level.

12. Explain how individuals can get involved in political party activities at the local level.

13. Illustrate the influence political party participants have on party platforms and issues, focusing on the pro-life issue at the Texas State Republican Convention.

14. Explain the philosophical differences between the two major political parties.

15. Explain the influence of third parties on the election process, and describe the impact of Ross Perot's Reform Party.

PRACTICE TEST

After reading the assignment, watching the video, and addressing the objectives, you should be able to complete the following Practice Test. Some essay questions in this Practice Test may be included in your exams. When you have completed the Practice Test, turn to the Answer Key to score your answers.

MULTIPLE CHOICE

Select the single best answer. If more than one answer is required, it will be so indicated.

1. Political parties perform which of the following functions?
   A. Provide an orderly succession to power
   B. Mobilize the demands and supports that are fed into the system
   C. Help hold officials accountable to the voters
   D. All of the above

2. Which of the following is true about the feelings that George Washington had toward political parties?
   A. In *The Federalist,* No. 10, he foresaw that Americans would group together into factions.
   B. He warned against the baneful effects of the spirit of party.
   C. He formed the Federalist Party.
   D. He formed the Democratic-Republican Party.

3. Which of the following depicts the origin of the Federalist Party?
   A. It was organized by Alexander Hamilton, stood for strong central government, and made its appeal to banking, commercial, and financial interests.
   B. It was organized by Thomas Jefferson and made its appeal to small farmers, debtors, and southern planters.
   C. It was organized by Henry Clay and Daniel Webster and appealed to those who detested Andrew Jackson.
   D. It was a northern sectional party that was formed to protest the expansion of slavery.

4. The party that was organized by Thomas Jefferson and that made its appeal to agrarian interests, debtors, and frontiersmen was the _____
   A. Democratic-Republican Party.
   B. Federalist Party.
   C. Whig Party.
   D. Populist Party.

5. Which of the following best defines the Democratic-Republican Party?
   A. It was a northern sectional party that was formed to protest the expansion of slavery.
   B. It was organized by Alexander Hamilton, favored a strong central government, and appealed to the urban, financial interests.
   C. It was an agrarian protest movement led by William Jennings Bryan that tied itself to the "free silver" movement.
   D. It was organized by Thomas Jefferson in an alliance with Aaron Burr that favored agrarian interests and appealed to debtors and frontiersmen.

6. The first Republican to be elected to the presidency was _____
   A. Andrew Jackson.
   B. Theodore Roosevelt.
   C. James Fremont.
   D. Abraham Lincoln.

7. Which independent candidate for president made the strongest showing since Theodore Roosevelt ran as the head of the Progressive ("Bull Moose") Party in 1912?
   A. George Wallace
   B. Eugene McCarthy
   C. Ross Perot
   D. John Anderson

8. Which type of electoral system appears to contribute to the formation of a two-party system in any society?
   A. Single-member districts where, in order to win, the candidate must receive a plurality of votes
   B. Single-member districts where, in order to win, the candidate must receive a majority of votes
   C. A multimember district where, in order to win, the candidate must receive a majority of votes
   D. A multimember district that uses the proportional representation method of selecting representatives for the legislative branch

9. Regarding the decline of party loyalty, which of the following is a correct statement?
   A. Political parties have become extinct in the United States.
   B. More people call themselves independents than call themselves Democrats and Republicans.
   C. More people call themselves Democrats and Republicans than call themselves independents.
   D. None of the above.

10. The fading of party loyalties among many voters has been one of the most visible features of American politics in recent years. Some of the reasons are _____
    A. a more educated electorate.
    B. an increase in "split-ticket" voting.
    C. the increased importance of television.
    D. all of the above.

11. A classic study of national convention delegates found that the opinions of Democratic and Republican leaders diverged sharply and that _____
    A. they were found to conform to party images.
    B. Republican leaders identified with big business, free enterprise, and economic conservation.
    C. Democrats were friendly toward labor and government regulation of the economy.
    D. all of the above.

12. Which of the following would most likely support a Democratic over a Republican candidate?
    A. A Catholic who lives in a big city in the North
    B. An African American who lives in a big city in the North
    C. A Polish American who lives in a large northern city, belongs to a union, drinks beer, and has a fairly low income
    D. All of the above

13. Which of the following would most likely vote for a Republican candidate?
    A. An African American who lives in a large northern city and who is a union member
    B. A white, Protestant corporate executive who resides in a suburb
    C. A Roman Catholic who resides in a large northern city and whose income is fairly low
    D. A Jewish American who lives in a large northern city and who works on an assembly line

14. Which of the following statements correctly describe the philosophies of the Republican or Democratic parties?
    A. Democrats tend to believe in the ability of government to solve problems.
    B. Republicans tend to believe in the inclusion of all relevant groups and viewpoints.
    C. Democrats tend to see themselves as insiders who represent the core of American society and as carriers of fundamental values.
    D. All of the above.

15. What do the Know-Nothings of the 1850s, the Populists of the 1890s, and the Progressives of the 1920s have in common?
    A. They were parties that appealed to large corporations.
    B. They were parties that appealed to labor unions.
    C. They were parties that resulted from agrarian unrest.
    D. They were third-party movements.

16. State parties are bound to the national party by _____
    A. law.
    B. strict discipline.
    C. a mutual desire to have a "winner" at the head of the ticket who can provide a "coattail" effect.
    D. ideology.

17. Which of the following has contributed to the decline of old-style, big-city political machines?
    A. Social Security
    B. General prosperity
    C. Unemployment benefits
    D. All of the above

18. Which of the following is true of the 1996 and 2000 national nominating conventions of both major parties?
    A. They were carefully scripted.
    B. They were made-for-television entertainments.
    C. They were designed by professional TV producers to appeal to prime-time audiences.
    D. All of the above.

19. Which of the following is true of the national conventions that have met since 1960?
    A. They have filled more of a selection function than a ratifying function.
    B. They have filled more of a ratifying function than a selection function.
    C. They have been a factional victory type.
    D. They have usually ended by selecting a "dark horse" or compromise candidate.

20. Although national conventions may no longer, as a rule, be an arena for political struggle, they still serve a purpose because _____
    A. they choose nominees for president and vice president.
    B. they provide a forum for the voters to see the nominees in action as they deliver their acceptance speeches.
    C. they may unify the party.
    D. all of the above.

21. According to Gerald M. Pomper _____
    A. political parties rarely carry out their campaign promises.
    B. political parties never carry out their campaign promises.
    C. political parties usually carry out their campaign promises.
    D. party platforms are meaningless.

22. Volunteers and party organizers can have the most access to and influence on party politics at the _____ level.
    A. local
    B. regional
    C. state
    D. national

23. It is important for everyone to be involved regardless of which side one is on, because if one doesn't participate _____
    A. somebody else will do the participating for you.
    B. one will be required to complete a community service project.
    C. one will be expected to contribute financially to a campaign.
    D. one will not be eligible to vote in a national referendum.

24. Tom Pauken holds the view that whether Democrat or Republican, we have to _____
    A. put the country first.
    B. contest the issues.
    C. solicit national support.
    D. play party politics.

25. The national chairperson of each party is chosen by _____
    A. popular vote of the general membership.
    B. majority vote of state chairs.
    C. national committee members of each party.
    D. general membership of each party.

26. In theory, it is the national chairperson's job to _____
    A. recruit the chair replacement for the next national convention.
    B. manage the presidential campaign.
    C. coordinate the governors' and mayors' national conferences.
    D. oversee the presidential debates.

27. The Reform Party has organized around all of the following issues EXCEPT _____
    A. balancing the national budget.
    B. passing public congressional campaign funding.
    C. reducing the national debt.
    D. requesting campaign finance reform.

ESSAY/PROBLEM QUESTIONS

28. Define *political parties*. Explain the functions that they perform in democratic governance.

29. Compare the philosophies of the two major political parties (Democrat and Republican) in the United States in regard to the role of government and on major issues. Describe the typical party identifiers of each party and explain how the differences in philosophy may result in the different groups identifying with each party. Are there any groups that might not be represented by one of the two major parties' philosophies?

30. Describe the recent trends in party identification among the U.S. public. Evaluate the political parties' perception that other institutions are taking over some of their roles in U.S. politics. In your opinion, how may the technological advances in the next few decades affect the role of political parties?

31. Discuss the pros and cons of political participation and nonparticipation in political parties. What are the most effective and important aspects of these activities?

32. Describe the issue that divided the Texas Republican Party at its state convention, and explain the effect this division had at the state and national conventions.

33. With which political party are you more closely aligned? Give specific reasons why you think you identify with that party.

ANSWER KEY

The following provides the answers and references for the Practice Test questions. Objectives are referenced using the following abbreviations:
T=Textbook Objectives   V=Video Objectives

1. D .... T1 .... Cummings, p. 250
2. B .... T2 .... Cummings, p. 251
3. A .... T2 .... Cummings, pp. 250–251
4. A .... T2 .... Cummings, p. 251
5. D .... T2 .... Cummings, p. 251
6. D .... T2 .... Cummings, p. 252
7. C .... T3, V15 .... Cummings, p. 254, Video
8. A .... T3 .... Cummings, p. 255
9. C .... T4 .... Cummings, p. 257
10. D .... T4 .... Cummings, p. 257
11. D .... T5 .... Cummings, p. 256
12. D .... T5 .... Cummings, p. 257
13. B .... T5 .... Cummings, p. 260
14. A .... T5, V14 .... Cummings, p. 258, Video
15. D .... T6 .... Cummings, p. 261
16. C .... T7 .... Cummings, p. 265
17. D .... T7 .... Cummings, p. 265
18. D .... T8 .... Cummings, p. 266
19. B .... T8 .... Cummings, p. 272
20. D .... T8 .... Cummings, p. 274
21. C .... T9 .... Cummings, p. 275
22. A .... V11 .... Video
23. A .... V12 .... Video
24. A .... V13 .... Video
25. C .... V14 .... Video
26. B .... V14 .... Video
27. B .... V15 .... Video
28. .... T1 .... Cummings, pp. 248–250
29. .... T5 .... Cummings, pp. 256–261
30. .... T4, T10 .... Cummings, pp. 256–257, p. 277
31. .... V12 .... Video
32. .... V13 .... Video
33. .... V14 .... Video

Lesson 11

Media and Elections

LESSON ASSIGNMENTS

Review the following assignments in order to schedule your time appropriately. Pay careful attention. The titles and numbers of the textbook chapter, the telecourse guide lesson, and the video program may be different from one another.

Text:

Cummings and Wise, *Democracy Under Pressure*, Chapter 8, "The Media and Politics," pp. 222–225 only.

Video:

"Media and Elections" from the series *Voices in Democracy: United States Government*.

Activities:

One or more activities may be assigned to this lesson. Refer to your syllabus.

OVERVIEW

This lesson examines the role of the media in providing information on elections to the public. We evaluate television as a source of information and evaluate its evolving impact on public opinion. Also we examine why and how regulation of the broadcast media is different from regulation of the print media and how this regulation shapes the broadcast media's options in presenting news and commentary.

We focus on the role of the media in providing information about candidates and the process of running for office. We also examine the interrelationship between candidates and the media. Media are essential to political campaigning and candidates. Reporting elections news is an important responsibility of the media.

LESSON GOAL

You should be able to explain the role media have played in the U.S. political campaigns throughout history and to discuss how a discerning voter can make an intelligent choice.

TEXTBOOK OBJECTIVES

The following objectives are designed to help you get the most from the text. Review them before reading the assignment. You may want to write notes to reinforce what you have learned.

1. Discuss complaints about television as a source of information, news, and entertainment. Evaluate television's impact on public opinion.

2. Discuss how television news, news magazines, and cable systems have revolutionized public access to information, particularly concerning international events and presidential campaigns.

3. Explain why it is that radio and television do not enjoy the same freedoms as the print media.

4. Discuss the ways in which the Federal Communications Commission (FCC) has regulated radio and television. Describe and evaluate the ways in which FCC regulation shapes the broadcast media's options in presenting news and commentary.

VIDEO OBJECTIVES

The following objectives are designed to help you get the most from the video segment of this lesson. Review them before watching the video. You may want to write notes to reinforce what you have learned.

5. Explain the role media have played in the U.S. political campaigns throughout history.

6. Describe the role political consultants play in today's campaigns.

7. Explain the relationship between the media and political campaigns from the viewpoint of media.

8. Discuss media's responsibility in covering the national party conventions and reporting results of polls.

9. Explain how third-party candidates use the media to benefit their campaigns.

10. Discuss how a discerning voter can make an intelligent choice.

PRACTICE TEST

After reading the assignment, watching the video, and addressing the objectives, you should be able to complete the following Practice Test. Some essay questions in this Practice Test may be included in your exams. When you have completed the Practice Test, turn to the Answer Key to score your answers.

MULTIPLE CHOICE

Select the single best answer. If more than one answer is required, it will be so indicated.

1. Which of the following types of programming represents the economic heart of the television industry?
   A. Entertainment
   B. News
   C. Public affairs
   D. Public policy

2. In a foreign policy crisis, which broadcast network often brings news to Washington faster than the government's secure communications channels?
   A. ABC
   B. CBS
   C. CNN
   D. NBC

3. The FCC requirement that radio and television broadcasters present all sides of public issues is called _____
   A. equal time doctrine.
   B. fairness doctrine.
   C. prior restraint.
   D. scarcity doctrine.

4. The primary source of campaign news in the United States is _____
   A. newspapers.
   B. political newsletters.
   C. radio.
   D. television.

5. A political consultant's responsibilities include all of the following to attract media attention EXCEPT _____
   A. polling.
   B. creating advertisements.
   C. writing legislation.
   D. designing special events.

6. According to Hal Bruno, journalists are sensitive to being stampeded into doing a story that would be destructive of another candidate, an action called _____
   A. spinning.
   B. photo op.
   C. speculation.
   D. manipulation.

7. The role of the press is to take the complex accumulation of information about the candidates and their positions on the issues and _____
   A. point the American public to the correct choice.
   B. help the American people make sense of them.
   C. keep the congressional leaders updated on their polls.
   D. eliminate the weak candidates and frivolous issues.

8. According to Russ Verney, a(n) _____ is an opportunity for a candidate to communicate directly to the public in an unfiltered way and provide them with information from a trusted and reliable source.
   A. political spin
   B. earned media
   C. infomercial
   D. political debate

9. Jim Fry believes that people should do things other than watch television to learn about candidates and issues; he urges interested people to _____
   A. attend rallies.
   B. interview candidates.
   C. read, read, read.
   D. write, write, write.

ESSAY/PROBLEM QUESTIONS

10. Describe how the evolution of media has revolutionized public access to information. Evaluate the role of the media in shaping opinion about national and international events.

11. Explain why television and radio do not enjoy the same freedoms as the print media. Think about the Internet. How is it similar or different from other news media? What level of regulation would be appropriate for it? Is it more like broadcast media or more like print media?

12. Discuss the ways in which the FCC has regulated radio and television. Describe and evaluate the ways in which the FCC regulations shape broadcast media options in presenting news and commentary.

13. What is the likelihood of media continuing to cover national party conventions? Why/Why not?

14. Explain the "horse race" coverage of political campaigns. How are the reporters providing information on presidential races to help people make voting choices?

15. Describe Ross Perot's campaigns. How do they differ from the norm? What are some of the methods he used to get on television which were different from previous elections, but were adopted by other presidential candidates? How did the Reform Party use the computer for voting for nominees at their convention? What new uses of the media do you think will be employed by candidates for president in 2004?

ANSWER KEY

The following provides the answers and references for the Practice Test questions. Objectives are referenced using the following abbreviations:
T=Textbook Objectives   V=Video Objectives

#	Ans	Obj	Reference
1.	A	T1	Cummings, p. 222
2.	C	T2	Cummings, pp. 222–223
3.	B	T3, T4	Cummings, pp. 224–225
4.	D	V5	Video
5.	C	V6	Video
6.	D	V7	Video
7.	B	V8	Video
8.	C	V9	Video
9.	C	V10	Video
10.		T1, T2	Cummings, pp. 216–221
11.		T4	Cummings, pp. 224–225
12.		T4	Cummings, pp. 224–225
13.		V8	Video
14.		V8	Video
15.		V9	Video

Lesson 12

Presidential Elections

LESSON ASSIGNMENTS

Review the following assignments in order to schedule your time appropriately. Pay careful attention. The titles and numbers of the textbook chapter, the telecourse guide lesson, and the video program may be different from one another.

Text:
> Cummings and Wise, *Democracy Under Pressure*, Chapter 10, "Political Campaigns and Candidates," pp. 281–323, and Chapter 11, "Voting Behavior and Elections," pp. 342–356 and "Counting the Votes," "Fraud," and "The Electoral College," pp. 361–363.

Video:
> "Presidential Elections" from the series *Voices in Democracy: United States Government*.

Activities:
> One or more activities may be assigned to this lesson. Refer to your syllabus.

OVERVIEW

This lesson examines the process of nominating and electing the U.S. president. Modern campaigns are evaluated in regard to their strategies and their impact on presidential elections. We also examine the impact that television, the evening news in particular, and Madison Avenue style advertising have on the strategies and cost of presidential campaigns. We also evaluate congressional attempts to reform campaign financing and identify the problems that still remain unsolved. The information in this lesson should help you to evaluate the role that money and modern campaigns play in contemporary democratic elections. By understanding the process of nominating and electing a president, including strategies employed to win the electoral college, you should have a better understanding when you vote.

LESSON GOAL

You should be able to discuss the importance of nominating and electing a U.S. president and to describe the major components and strategies of each election, including media, polling, and fund raising.

TEXTBOOK OBJECTIVES

The following objectives are designed to help you get the most from the text. Review them before reading the assignment. You may want to write notes to reinforce what you have learned.

1. Describe the organization of modern campaigns and discuss the major goals and strategies of presidential campaigns.

2. Describe the role issues play in campaigns and discuss the strategies of campaigns to deal with issues. Compare the roles of bread-and-butter issues with foreign policy issues in presidential campaigns.

3. Examine the role of television in presidential campaigns. Discuss the impact of presidential debates from the 1960s to the present.

4. Describe the role of Madison Avenue techniques and the role of professional campaign managers.

5. Examine the role of the news media in shaping political campaigns.

6. Examine recent trends in the cost of presidential campaigns. Describe recent attempts to regulate campaign finance. Evaluate the roles of federal campaign funding, PACs, and soft money in presidential campaigns.

7. Evaluate the roles that money and campaigns play in democratic societies. Identify problems that remain to be solved.

8. Describe the 2000 presidential election in terms of the selection of candidates and the development of strategies in the general campaign.

9. Describe and evaluate the electoral college system.

VIDEO OBJECTIVES

The following objectives are designed to help you get the most from the video segment of this lesson. Review them before watching the video. You may want to write notes to reinforce what you have learned.

10. Discuss the importance of nominating and electing a U.S. president.

11. Describe the activities in which each candidate must participate to mount a viable candidacy for the presidency and survive the primary elections.

12. Describe the major strategies for winning in the primary season.

13. Describe the campaign strategies for the November presidential election, including the importance of the electoral college and presidential debates.

PRACTICE TEST

After reading the assignment, watching the video, and addressing the objectives, you should be able to complete the following Practice Test. Some essay questions in this Practice Test may be included in your exams. When you have completed the Practice Test, turn to the Answer Key to score your answers.

MULTIPLE CHOICE

Select the single best answer. If more than one answer is required, it will be so indicated.

1. If elections are decided by "ticket-splitters," as DeVries and Tarrance contend, campaigns should be used to _____
   A. communicate the candidate's views on issues.
   B. project the candidate's personality.
   C. personally attack the opposing candidate.
   D. preserve the candidate's party base.

2. A pivotal state is _____
   A. a large, populous state with many electoral votes that a candidate must win to be elected.
   B. a state that frequently changes party allegiance.
   C. a state that always supports one party.
   D. a state that always supports the incumbent president.

3. Negative campaigning is when candidates engage in _____
   A. taking the lofty, nonpartisan approach.
   B. discussing the issues and not personalities.
   C. making personal attacks on their opponents.
   D. attempting to change the minds of the voters.

4. Voters have tended to associate the Republicans with _____
   A. social progress at home.
   B. prosperity.
   C. success in foreign policy.
   D. all of the above.

5. In 1988, when George Bush ran against Michael Dukakis, he campaigned as _____
   A. a candidate of the "out" party.
   B. an incumbent president.
   C. the political heir of an incumbent president.
   D. none of the above.

6. Why do candidates try to sell themselves and their ideas on television?
   A. They are required by federal statute to do so.
   B. It is the surest means of reaching the largest number of people.
   C. It is the safest means, although it doesn't reach as many people as personal campaigning.
   D. It is cheaper than traveling throughout the country to personally meet the voters.

7. With regard to the Carter-Reagan televised debates _____
   A. Carter was able to convince the voters that the Republican nominee was an aggressive hawk who might lead the country into war.
   B. Carter was able to convince the voters that the Republican nominee would ruin the economy of the country.
   C. Reagan was able to offset Carter's warnings that he was an aggressive hawk who might lead the country into war.
   D. Reagan was able to win due to Carter's physical appearance.

8. Which of the following is a concern related to the increased use of television and Madison Avenue techniques in political campaigns?
   A. That only actors would be good political candidates
   B. That political candidates could be packaged and merchandised like toothpaste
   C. That only Madison Avenue executives would be good political candidates
   D. There are no concerns

9. One of the results of the increased use of television and Madison Avenue techniques in political campaigns has been _____
   A. lowering the cost of campaigns because there is less travel for the candidates.
   B. strengthening party discipline, especially at the state and local levels.
   C. raising the cost of campaigns because this is a very expensive way to campaign.
   D. none of the above.

10. Patterson and McClure argue that the impact of the nightly network newscasts on political campaigns has been to _____
    A. distort and trivialize them.
    B. explain and simplify them so the average voter is able to make an intelligent choice.
    C. concentrate on the issues, thereby serving campaigns in a highly positive manner.
    D. point out when candidates are engaging in negative campaigns and therefore should be ignored.

11. During the 1992 campaign, which candidate had the most press time spent on issues that were negative for him?
    A. Bill Clinton
    B. George Bush
    C. Ross Perot
    D. The press spent equal time on all three

12. The first major party candidates for president to finance their election campaigns with federal funds were _____
    A. John Kennedy and Richard Nixon in 1960.
    B. Hubert Humphrey and Richard Nixon in 1968.
    C. Jimmy Carter and Gerald Ford in 1976.
    D. George Bush and Bill Clinton in 1992.

13. Funds raised by the major parties that are not subject to the limits of federal law and that are spent by the parties in the states to indirectly aid candidates are _____
    A. soft money.
    B. independent expenditures.
    C. illegal under the Federal Election Campaign Act.
    D. illegal according to the Supreme Court in *Buckley v. Valeo.*

14. In a TV commercial for a presidential candidate in 2000, a female announcer attacked his major opponent's prescription drug plan, school accountability plan, and targeted tax cuts. Who was the candidate who ran this commercial?
    A. Pat Buchanan
    B. Al Gore
    C. George W. Bush
    D. Ralph Nader

15. Electoral votes are allocated to a state _____
    A. by the Supreme Court.
    B. based upon the number of representatives the state has in Congress.
    C. based upon the number of representatives the state has in the House of Representatives.
    D. based upon the voter turnout in that state in the previous election.

16. Which of the following is correct regarding the selection of electors?
    A. The Constitution established that they must be selected by popular vote in all states.
    B. A federal statute established that they must be selected by popular vote in all states.
    C. The Supreme Court established that they must be selected by popular vote in all states.
    D. Legally, a state may select them any way that it wishes.

17. Which of the following are arguments used by those who oppose abolition of the electoral college in favor of the direct popular election of the president?
    A. It would increase the temptation for fraud in vote counting, leading to prolonged recounts and chaos.
    B. It would rob minority groups of their influence in big electoral-vote states.
    C. It would tempt states to ease voter qualification standards in order to fatten the voter rolls.
    D. All of the above.

18. The most important prerogative(s) of a citizen is/are the right to _____
    A. attend a presidential debate and question the candidates.
    B. go to the polls to choose those who govern the country.
    C. hold an elective office.
    D. all of the above.

19. Once a person decides to become a presidential candidate, serious planning, organizing, and fund-raising must begin at least _____
    A. three months before the general election.
    B. six months before the general election.
    C. one year before the general election.
    D. two years before the general election.

20. The main thing that presidents can do in order to dissuade opponents within their own party is to _____
    A. be a long-time party member.
    B. have many years of political experience.
    C. be popular.
    D. be wealthy.

21. Traditionally, the first major events of the primary season are the _____
    A. Iowa caucuses and the New York primary.
    B. Iowa caucuses and the New Hampshire primary.
    C. Indiana caucuses and the New England primary.
    D. Indiana caucuses and the New Hampshire primary.

Lesson 12—Presidential Elections

22. In order to win the November general election, a presidential candidate must
    A. win a majority of the popular vote.
    B. win a majority of the electoral votes.
    C. win in thirty-five of the fifty states.
    D. reach a financial threshold in twenty-six states.

23. The general election campaign tends disproportionately to be fought out in states with
    A. large numbers of electoral votes.
    B. large political party membership.
    C. strong union activities.
    D. major financial institutions.

24. In addition to people needing to understand and see that they have a stake in an election, the presidential debates also allow
    A. candidates to point out their strengths and challenges.
    B. ordinary people to ask extraordinary questions.
    C. congressional leaders to evaluate a possible adversary.
    D. contributors to see how they have invested their funds.

ESSAY/PROBLEM QUESTIONS

25. Define and give examples of *negative campaigning*, *bread-and-butter issues*, and *foreign policy issues*. Describe how presidential campaigns might choose to deal strategically with these issues.

26. Define *soft money* and *independent expenditures*. Describe recent trends regarding these two types of campaign contributions. Explain why public funding of presidential campaigns has not eliminated these two types of contributions. Do you think that attempts to curb these types of expenditures would be unconstitutionally limiting freedom of speech? Justify your answer.

27. Explain the events of the 2000 presidential election. What were the major issues for each party? What impact did third parties have on the outcome? What impact did the debates have? Identify the controversies over counting the ballots and how this affected the electoral outcome.

28. Why should individuals become involved and vote in presidential elections? What are the important aspects of presidential elections an interested voter should know and understand?

29. Explain the difference between a primary election and a general election.

30. What was the significance of Ross Perot's 1992 and 1996 campaigns in the presidential elections?

31. How important are presidential debates to the general elections? Explain.

ANSWER KEY

#	Answer	Reference	Source
1.	A	T1	Cummings, p. 291
2.	A	T1	Cummings, pp. 292–293
3.	C	T1, T2	Cummings, p. 296
4.	C	T2	Cummings, p. 297
5.	C	T2	Cummings, p. 295
6.	B	T3	Cummings, p. 282
7.	C	T3	Cummings, pp. 301–304
8.	B	T4	Cummings, p. 306
9.	C	T4	Cummings, p. 306
10.	A	T5, V11	Cummings, p. 307, Video
11.	A	T5	Cummings, p. 312
12.	C	T6, T7	Cummings, p. 313
13.	A	T6, T7	Cummings, p. 315
14.	C	T8	Cummings, pp. 281–282
15.	B	T9, V13	Cummings, p. 362, Video
16.	D	T9	Cummings, p. 363
17.	D	T9	Cummings, p. 363
18.	D	V10	Video
19.	D	V11	Video
20.	C	V11	Video
21.	B	V12	Video
22.	B	V13	Video
23.	A	V13	Video
24.	B	V13	Video
25.		T2	Cummings, pp. 295–301
26.		T6, T7	Cummings, pp. 313–321
27.		T8, T9	(Cummings, pp. 342-356)
28.		V10, V13	Video
29.		V12, V13	Video
30.		V13	Video
31.		V13	Video

Lesson 13

Congressional Elections

LESSON ASSIGNMENTS

Review the following assignments in order to schedule your time appropriately. Pay careful attention. The titles and numbers of the textbook chapter, the telecourse guide lesson, and the video program may be different from one another.

Text:
> Cummings and Wise, *Democracy Under Pressure*, Chapter 11, "Voting Behavior and Elections," pp. 337–342, pp. 359–361, and pp. 364–368 only.

Video:
> "Congressional Elections" from the series *Voices in Democracy: United States Government*.

Activities:
> One or more activities may be assigned to this lesson. Refer to your syllabus.

OVERVIEW

This lesson takes a closer look at a set of issues concerning elections. First, differences in congressional races during presidential and midterm elections are explored. Second, the impact of voter registration requirements and ballots are examined. Third, the issue of reapportionment is evaluated, particularly in light of Supreme Court rulings on equal representation in the 1960s and minority protected districts in the 1990s. The impact of elections on public policy is also considered. Congressional elections and candidate strategies vary depending upon geographical locations, safe seats (either Democrat or Republican) and house versus senate campaigns.

LESSON GOAL

You should be able to explain the importance of congressional elections and to describe the major aspects of congressional campaigning including funding, media exposure, and use of volunteers.

TEXTBOOK OBJECTIVES

The following objectives are designed to help you get the most from the text. Review them before reading the assignment. You may want to write notes to reinforce what you have learned.

1. Discuss the general differences between voter trends for congressional elections in midterm elections and presidential elections.

2. Define the terms *coalitions* and *coattails*. Give examples of each in recent elections.

3. Examine the typical state legal requirements for registering to vote. Evaluate how these requirements may affect voter turnout in the United States.

4. Distinguish between party-column ballots and office-column ballots. Describe and evaluate recent attempts to make voting easier for citizens.

5. Define *reapportionment*. Discuss the Supreme Court cases *Baker v. Carr, Reynolds v. Sims,* and *Wesberry v. Sanders* in relation to the question of equal representation.

6. Examine and evaluate the issue of drawing congressional districts to protect minority influence, especially in light of recent Supreme Court rulings.

7. Explain the impact that elections can have on public policy.

VIDEO OBJECTIVES

The following objectives are designed to help you get the most from the video segment of this lesson. Review them before watching the video. You may want to write notes to reinforce what you have learned.

8. Explain the importance of congressional elections.

9. Examine the major aspects of congressional campaigning.

10. Discuss some of the common concerns that people want their congressional delegates to address.

11. Explain the importance of fund-raising in congressional races and list several fund-raising strategies.

12. Compare and contrast the campaign strategies used in different states.

PRACTICE TEST

After reading the assignment, watching the video, and addressing the objectives, you should be able to complete the following Practice Test. Some essay questions in this Practice Test may be included in your exams. When you have completed the Practice Test, turn to the Answer Key to score your answers.

MULTIPLE CHOICE

Select the single best answer. If more than one answer is required, it will be so indicated.

1. Which of the following is correct concerning voting behavior in presidential and congressional elections from 1932 to 1992?
   A. There is no difference in voting behavior in presidential elections and congressional elections.
   B. Since the end of World War II the Democratic Party has been stronger in presidential elections than in congressional elections.
   C. Since the end of World War II the Democratic Party has been stronger in congressional elections than in presidential elections.
   D. Since the end of World War II the Republican Party has been stronger in congressional elections than in presidential elections.

2. Which of the following statements concerning midterm or off-year elections is correct?
   A. The president's party generally loses strength in midterm congressional elections.
   B. Substantially fewer voters turn out in off-year elections.
   C. Substantially fewer peripheral voters turn out in off-year elections than in presidential elections.
   D. All of the above.

3. Alliances of segments of the electorate who coalesce behind a political candidate are _____
   A. coalitions.
   B. coattail effects.
   C. split tickets.
   D. checkerboard effects.

4. Which of the following states uses roving canvassers to remind people to vote?
   A. Kansas
   B. New York
   C. California
   D. Idaho

5. A party-column ballot _____
   A. encourages straight-party voting.
   B. lists the candidates of each party in a row or column beside or under the party name.
   C. is also called the Indiana ballot.
   D. all of the above.

6. The redrawing of congressional districts following the census is called _____
   A. incumbency effect.
   B. gerrymandering.
   C. reapportionment.
   D. electioneering.

7. *Reynolds v. Sims* and *Wesberry v. Sanders* established _____
   A. one person, one vote.
   B. both congressional and state districts must be equally proportioned.
   C. only state districts must be equally proportioned.
   D. both A and B.

8. In a series of decisions concerning the drawing of congressional districts, the U.S. Supreme Court ruled that _____
   A. several districts that were drawn to protect Republicans in Texas and North Carolina were unconstitutional.
   B. several districts that were drawn to protect minority-group voters were unconstitutional.
   C. congressional districts must be apportioned equally between rural and urban populations.
   D. Congress could not require states to redraw districts.

9. According to V. O. Key, Jr., one of the most fundamental ways by which people can influence government is through _____
   A. financial contributions.
   B. grass-roots pressure.
   C. voting.
   D. electioneering.

10. There are _____ members of the U.S. House of Representatives.
    A. 100
    B. 435
    C. 535
    D. 630

11. _____ is/are the key to getting the message to as many voters as possible.
    A. Numbers
    B. Media
    C. Travel
    D. Personality

12. Which of the following is NOT a concern that the citizens of Chicago want their congressional representatives to address?
    A. The trade deficit
    B. The care of senior citizens
    C. The welfare situation we have today
    D. Kids to stay in school

13. Which of the following does NOT describe the fund-raising strategies of Victor Morales' congressional campaign?
    A. Mr. Morales did not take PAC contributions.
    B. Mr. Morales out-raised Mr. Gramm 14–1.
    C. Mr. Morales raised $900,000 in four to five months.
    D. Eighty-six percent of his funds were in increments of $100 or less.

14. In developing a candidate's schedule, the trick is to _____
    A. get the candidate before as many voters in as little time as possible.
    B. set up appearances only before large audiences of registered voters.
    C. choose only those communities that have pledged their support to the candidate.
    D. focus on the issues that the opponent has ignored.

ESSAY/PROBLEM QUESTIONS

15. Describe the different levels of voter requirements across the various states. Evaluate how voter requirements affect voter turnout. Describe recent national and state attempts to make it easier for voters both to register and to vote.

16. Describe fully the reapportionment process for Congress. Discuss and evaluate the Supreme Court's impact on this process in the 1960s and in the 1990s.

17. What makes congressional elections so important to the political process?

18. List the major components of congressional campaigns and explain their functions.

19. Analyze the campaign styles of the various congressional candidates in Montana, Chicago, and Texas.

ANSWER KEY

The following provides the answers and references for the Practice Test questions. Objectives are referenced using the following abbreviations:

T=Textbook Objectives   V=Video Objectives

1.	C	T1	Cummings, p. 338
2.	D	T1	Cummings, pp. 340–341
3.	A	T2	Cummings, p. 337
4.	D	T3	Cummings, p. 359
5.	D	T4	Cummings, p. 360
6.	C	T5	Cummings, p. 364
7.	D	T5	Cummings, pp. 364–365
8.	B	T6	Cummings, p. 366
9.	C	T7, T8	Cummings, p. 368
10.	C	V8	Video
11.	B	V9	Video
12.	A	V10	Video
13.	B	V11	Video
14.	A	V12	Video
15.		T3, T4	Cummings, pp. 359–361
16.		T5, T6	Cummings, pp. 364–366
17.		V8	Video
18.		V9	Video
19.		V12	Video

Lesson 14

Congress

LESSON ASSIGNMENTS

Review the following assignments in order to schedule your time appropriately. Pay careful attention. The titles and numbers of the textbook chapter, the telecourse guide lesson, and the video program may be different from one another.

Text:
Cummings and Wise, *Democracy Under Pressure*, Chapter 12, "The Congress," pp. 373–405.

Video:
"Congress" from the series *Voices in Democracy: United States Government*.

Activities:
One or more activities may be assigned to this lesson. Refer to your syllabus.

OVERVIEW

This lesson examines the U.S. Congress. The impact of the 1994 congressional elections, which resulted in Republican majorities in Congress, is discussed. The lesson then evaluates some of the conflicts and crises with which Congress has dealt—sometimes successfully and sometimes not. We also examine the ability of Congress to adapt and reform itself. The lesson discusses the varied roles that Congress plays in the public policy process and it explores the different and often conflicting roles of representation that a member of Congress may follow. Finally, this lesson examines the structure and function of the committee system and the congressional leadership in both houses of Congress and their impact on the legislative process.

LESSON GOAL

You should be able to describe the organization of the U.S. Congress, its leadership structure, and committee system.

TEXTBOOK OBJECTIVES

The following objectives are designed to help you get the most from the text. Review them before reading the assignment. You may want to write notes to reinforce what you have learned.

1. Discuss the importance of the 1994 congressional elections in light of the new GOP majorities in each house.

2. Discuss some of the controversies and conflicts in which Congress has been involved. Evaluate Congress' ability to deal with these issues and recent attempts to reform and modernize itself.

3. Describe the key roles that Congress plays.

4. Describe the background of typical members of Congress.

5. Distinguish between the trustee role and instructed delegate roles of representation and describe how members balance these roles.

6. Describe the committee system and formal leadership of the House and the Senate.

VIDEO OBJECTIVES

The following objectives are designed to help you get the most from the video segment of this lesson. Review them before watching the video. You may want to write notes to reinforce what you have learned.

7. Compare the makeup of Congress with the U.S. population as a whole.

8. Explain the leadership structure of Congress and the operation of congressional committees.

9. Describe the varied roles a member of Congress must play.

PRACTICE TEST

After reading the assignment, watching the video, and addressing the objectives, you should be able to complete the following Practice Test. Some essay questions in this Practice Test may be included in your exams. When you have completed the Practice Test, turn to the Answer Key to score your answers.

MULTIPLE CHOICE

Select the single best answer. If more than one answer is required, it will be so indicated.

1. As a result of the 1994 Republican congressional victory, which of the following became speaker of the House?
   A. Representative Tom DeLay
   B. Representative Dick Armey
   C. Representative Newt Gingrich
   D. Representative Charlie Rangel

2. By passing the War Powers Resolution, Congress was attempting to reassert its authority in _____
   A. the budgetary process.
   B. committing troops to combat overseas.
   C. the domestic policy process.
   D. the legislative process.

3. Which of the following is a function of Congress?
   A. Lawmaking
   B. Declaring war
   C. Regulating the conduct of its members and punishing them by censure or expulsion
   D. All of the above

4. Which of the following gives a senator of the president's party an informal veto over presidential appointments in that senator's state?
   A. Systems maintenance
   B. The power of the purse
   C. Senatorial courtesy
   D. The lawmaking function

5. The average age of members of the House of Representatives in the 106th Congress when it convened in January 1999 was _____
   A. fifty-five years.
   B. forty-three years.
   C. forty-five years.
   D. fifty-two years.

6. More than half of the nation's population are women. What percentage of the 106th Congress were women?
   A. 5 percent
   B. 12.5 percent
   C. 15 percent
   D. About 25 percent

7. How many African Americans served in the 106th Congress, with all but one being a member of the House of Representatives?
   A. Thirty-one
   B. Thirty-five
   C. Thirty-eight
   D. Thirty-nine

8. A representative whose vote automatically mirrors the will of a majority of her/his constituents is acting as _____
   A. an instructed delegate.
   B. a trustee.
   C. a Burkean disciple.
   D. none of the above.

9. Which of the following is in a position to block the passage of legislation by virtue of having power to control the flow of legislation to the floor of the House of Representatives?
   A. The speaker of the House
   B. The House Rules Committee
   C. The minority floor leader
   D. The majority floor leader

10. Which of the following is true regarding the speaker of the House?
    A. The position of speaker is provided for by the Constitution.
    B. The speaker has the power to preside over the House.
    C. The speaker has the power to recognize or ignore members who wish to speak.
    D. All of the above.

11. Which of the following positions in the Senate is most influential in determining the policy of that body?
    A. President of the Senate
    B. President pro tempore
    C. Speaker of the Senate
    D. Majority leader

12. Which of the following is considered a desirable committee assignment in the Senate?
    A. Rules Committee
    B. Ways and Means Committee
    C. Foreign Relations Committee
    D. All of the above

13. If a bill is passed by both houses but is not in identical language, it is sent to which of the following in an attempt to iron out the differences?
    A. A standing committee
    B. A select committee
    C. A conference committee
    D. The president

14. Oklahoma Representative J. C. Watts states that a person running for elective office should be motivated for all the following reasons EXCEPT _____
    A. getting involved in public service.
    B. trying to make a difference.
    C. getting elected for the salary.
    D. feeling like one can make a difference.

15. The chair of a congressional standing committee is determined by the _____
    A. speaker.
    B. majority leader.
    C. majority party.
    D. minority party.

16. Representative Tom DeLay, the majority whip, plays two roles: one is a national role and the second is to _____
    A. secure a leadership role.
    B. represent the people of one's district and state.
    C. earn an appointment by the major political party.
    D. influence legislation for the special interest groups.

17. Rounding up the votes to pass the legislation that the majority party in Congress wants is the principal job of the _____
    A. minority whip.
    B. majority whip.
    C. committee chair.
    D. speaker.

18. Members of the House of Representatives and Senate do far more than _____
    A. their counterparts in the executive branch.
    B. is expected of the judicial branch.
    C. all the civil servants in the bureaucracy.
    D. make laws.

ESSAY/PROBLEM QUESTIONS

19. List and discuss two issues that have been used to make a case against Congress. List and discuss two issues that have been used to make a case for Congress. Evaluate the legitimacy of these two viewpoints.

20. Describe the characteristics of a typical member of Congress. Compare these characteristics with those of the public at large, and evaluate the impact of these differences on democratic governance.

21. Compare the leadership positions in the House and the Senate. Explain their power and responsibilities in each house.

22. Does Congress reflect the population of the United States as a whole? Explain your answer. Describe your Congress member and the Senators from your state.

23. Describe the varied activities in which a member of Congress may be participating.

24. How can citizens become involved in the legislative process? Explain the activities available to influence that process. Give examples.

ANSWER KEY

The following provides the answers and references for the Practice Test questions. Objectives are referenced using the following abbreviations:

T=Textbook Objectives   V=Video Objectives

#	Answer	Objective	Reference
1.	C	T1	Cummings, p. 374
2.	B	T2	Cummings, p. 400
3.	D	T3	Cummings, pp. 377–378
4.	C	T3	Cummings, p. 378
5.	D	T4	Cummings, p. 379
6.	B	T4	Cummings, p. 379
7.	D	T4	Cummings, p. 379
8.	A	T5	Cummings, p. 382
9.	B	T6	Cummings, p. 386
10.	D	T6	Cummings, p. 385
11.	D	T6	Cummings, p. 390
12.	C	T6	Cummings, p. 394
13.	C	T6	Cummings, pp. 399–400
14.	C	V8	Video
15.	C	V8	Video
16.	B	V8	Video
17.	B	V8	Video
18.	D	V9	Video
19.		T2	Cummings, pp. 375–379
20.		T4, V7	Cummings, pp. 379–382, Video
21.		T6	Cummings, pp. 385–386, pp. 390–391
22.		V7	Video
23.		V8	Video
24.		V9	Video

Lesson 15

Legislative Process

LESSON ASSIGNMENTS

Review the following assignments in order to schedule your time appropriately. Pay careful attention. The titles and numbers of the textbook chapter, the telecourse guide lesson, and the video program may be different from one another.

Text:
> Cummings and Wise, *Democracy Under Pressure*, Chapter 12, "The Congress," pp. 383–393 and pp. 399–402 only, and Chapter 10, "Political Campaigns and Candidates," pp. 313–321 only.

Video:
> "Legislative Process" from the series *Voices in Democracy: United States Government*.

Activities:
> One or more activities may be assigned to this lesson. Refer to your syllabus.

OVERVIEW

This lesson focuses narrowly on the legislative process. The differences between the House and the Senate are described and the key differences in the processes of the two chambers are examined in detail. We also provide a general overview of the steps that are necessary for a bill to become a law. And a specific legislative tool—the legislative veto—and its fate in the courts is examined.

To illustrate the legislative process in action, the Assault Weapons Ban Bill and the McCain-Feingold Campaign Finance Reform Bill are examined. Besides knowing the general steps to passing a bill, it is important to understand the parliamentary procedures and political action used to either defeat or pass particular legislation.

LESSON GOAL

List the factors that influence the types of bills introduced in Congress, outline the major steps a bill must pass in becoming law, and describe the political process in which individuals and groups can affect the outcome.

TEXTBOOK OBJECTIVES

The following objectives are designed to help you get the most from the text. Review them before reading the assignment. You may want to write notes to reinforce what you have learned.

1. Describe the major differences between the House and the Senate.

2. Describe the House Rules Committee's function. Identify the House calendars and describe briefly their functions.

3. Define the terms *unanimous consent* and *filibuster* and describe how they make the process of legislation in the Senate different from the House.

4. Give an overview of the basic steps involved in making a bill become a law.

5. Define *legislative veto*. Discuss the Supreme Court's ruling on the legislative veto and subsequent presidential and congressional actions in regard to the legislative veto.

6. Describe recent attempts to reform campaign finance.

VIDEO OBJECTIVES

The following objectives are designed to help you get the most from the video segment of this lesson. Review them before watching the video. You may want to write notes to reinforce what you have learned.

7. Explain the factors that influence the types of bills offered as bills, and outline the major steps a bill must pass in becoming law.

8. Describe in detail the factors that influenced the progress of the Assault Weapons Ban Bill through the legislative process.

9. Describe the political battles involving campaign finance reform and the McCain-Feingold bill. Explain the difficulties this reform has encountered throughout the legislative process.

PRACTICE TEST

After reading the assignment, watching the video, and addressing the objectives, you should be able to complete the following Practice Test. Some essay questions in this Practice Test may be included in your exams. When you have completed the Practice Test, turn to the Answer Key to score your answers.

MULTIPLE CHOICE

Select the single best answer. If more than one answer is required, it will be so indicated.

1. Which of the following is true regarding the present relationship of the two houses of Congress?
    A. House seats are safer than Senate seats.
    B. Senate seats are safer than House seats.
    C. There are fewer marginal Senate seats than there are marginal House seats.
    D. The House is more responsive than the Senate to pressures for change in the status quo.

2. Which committee controls what bills are brought to the floor of the House of Representatives?
    A. The Ways and Means Committee
    B. The Rules Committee
    C. The Appropriations Committee
    D. The Conference Committee

3. An attempt to talk a bill to death and thus prevent it from coming to a vote in the Senate is a _____
   A. discharge petition.
   B. motion of cloture.
   C. special rule.
   D. filibuster.

4. How many votes are required to invoke a cloture in the Senate?
   A. Three-fifths of the entire Senate
   B. Sixty members
   C. It's too difficult to get
   D. Both A and B

5. In the *Chadha* case the Supreme Court ruled that _____
   A. the legislative veto is unconstitutional.
   B. the use of the Congressional Budget Office is unconstitutional.
   C. the use of the General Accounting Office to monitor executive spending is unconstitutional.
   D. the use of the Office of Technology Assessment is an invasion of the executive domain and therefore is unconstitutional.

6. Every year, each bill introduced in the U.S. Congress is an attempt to establish _____
   A. a rule of law governing some aspect of our lives.
   B. a seniority system to schedule time for floor debate.
   C. the means by which a freshman member of Congress may debate bills on the floor.
   D. the guidelines for a bill's first reading on the floor.

7. Which of the following is NOT an option for the president when Congress sends a bill to the White House?
   A. The president must take the bill to Congress to explain his views of the bill.
   B. The president can sign the bill and it becomes law.
   C. The president can veto the bill and send it back to Congress.
   D. The president can do nothing and the bill becomes law after ten days.

8. Which of the following was NOT a provision in the 1993 Assault Weapons Ban Bill?
   A. It banned nineteen kinds of assault weapons.
   B. It banned the making of ammunition clips holding more than ten rounds.
   C. It required a six-month period to check the records of the purchaser.
   D. It banned the importation of certain ammunition clips.

9. Opponents of the Assault Weapons Ban Bill claimed that the use of assault weapons in defending oneself and others _____
   A. should play an important role in the decision for members of Congress.
   B. required more hard data before voting.
   C. was greatly exaggerated.
   D. was proved statistically valid by police for stopping crime.

10. Senator John McCain states that average U.S. citizens are cynical and feel alienated about their ability to influence their government because they believe that special interests _____
    A. have bought access and influence.
    B. outnumber involved citizens.
    C. know more about the legislative process.
    D. are more likely to nominate their members for political office.

11. Senator Mitchell McConnell opposed the Campaign Finance Reform Bill because he believed it _____
    A. distracted from more seriously needed reforms.
    B. discouraged the average citizen from seeking political office.
    C. violated the First Amendment freedom of speech.
    D. confused proposed legislation by Common Cause.

ESSAY/PROBLEM QUESTIONS

12. Discuss three differences between the Senate and the House. Evaluate whether these differences make one house more suitable for democratic governance than the other.

13. Discuss the use of the filibuster and the measures available for ending a filibuster in the Senate. Give an example of an actual filibuster. Evaluate the appropriateness of such tactics in a democratic government.

14. Describe briefly the key steps that lead to a bill becoming a law.

15. Describe attempts to reform campaign finance prior to 1996. In what ways did those reforms fall short? Identify the key problems that remain to be solved.

16. What were the pros and cons of the assault weapons legislation? Which interest groups were the major players, and what stance did each group take?

17. Describe the legislative battle surrounding the McCain-Feingold bill, which dealt with campaign finance reform. What were some of the interesting political and parliamentary procedures used?

ANSWER KEY

The following provides the answers and references for the Practice Test questions. Objectives are referenced using the following abbreviations:

T=Textbook Objectives   V=Video Objectives

#	Ans	Obj	Reference
1.	A	T1	Cummings, p. 384
2.	B	T2	Cummings, p. 386
3.	D	T3	Cummings, p. 391
4.	D	T3	Cummings, p. 392
5.	A	T5	Cummings, p. 400
6.	A	V7	Video
7.	A	V7	Video
8.	C	V8	Video
9.	A	V8	Video
10.	A	V9	Video
11.	C	V9	Video
12.		T1	Cummings, pp. 383–393
13.		T3	Cummings, pp. 391–393
14.		T4, V7	Cummings, pp. 399–400, Video
15.		T6	Cummings, pp. 316–321
16.		V8	Video
17.		V9	Video

Lesson 16

Congress and the President

LESSON ASSIGNMENTS

Review the following assignments in order to schedule your time appropriately. Pay careful attention. The titles and numbers of the textbook chapter, the telecourse guide lesson, and the video program may be different from one another.

Text:
>Cummings and Wise, *Democracy Under Pressure*, Chapter 12, "The Congress," pp. 373–379 only, and Chapter 13, "The President," pp. 424–427, ("Chief Legislator" only).

Video:
>"Congress and the President" from the series *Voices in Democracy: United States Government*.

Activities:
>One or more activities may be assigned to this lesson. Refer to your syllabus.

OVERVIEW

This lesson explores the relationship between Congress and the president. The 1994 elections provide an illustration of the contemporary conflict between these two branches as they struggle for dominance in the policymaking arena. We examine the various roles played by Congress and the president and identify the separate and overlapping powers enjoyed by both in the legislative process. And we examine more closely the historical conflict that has often surfaced due to these shared powers.

In particular, we examine the struggle over the budget and the sending of troops to battle. Although a cooperative relationship is desired, conflict is more likely, especially when we have one political party dominating Congress and the president coming from the other major party. When different political parties control each of these two branches of government, we call it a divided government. And we have had a divided government for most of the last fifty years.

LESSON GOAL

Examine the strategy and powers that are unique to the president and to Congress as they interact with each other addressing the nation's business.

TEXTBOOK OBJECTIVES

The following objectives are designed to help you get the most from the text. Review them before reading the assignment. You may want to write notes to reinforce what you have learned.

1. Define and discuss divided government and the problems that can result from it. Evaluate how the elections of 1994 affected the relationship between President Clinton and Congress.

2. Describe the key roles that Congress plays in the policymaking process.

3. Describe the legislative powers and specific legislative tools of the president.

4. Discuss ways that uses of presidential power create conflict with Congress. Illustrate the conflict with recent examples.

VIDEO OBJECTIVES

The following objectives are designed to help you get the most from the video segment of this lesson. Review them before watching the video. You may want to write notes to reinforce what you have learned.

5. Explain possible philosophical conflicts between a president of one political party and a congressional majority of another party.

6. Using the example of the 1995–96 government shut down, explain the conflict between the president and Congress that usually develops with the budgeting process.

7. Describe the frequent conflict between the president and Congress over the deployment of military troops.

PRACTICE TEST

After reading the assignment, watching the video, and addressing the objectives, you should be able to complete the following Practice Test. Some essay questions in this Practice Test may be included in your exams. When you have completed the Practice Test, turn to the Answer Key to score your answers.

MULTIPLE CHOICE

Select the single best answer. If more than one answer is required, it will be so indicated.

1. Who got most of the blame over the battle of the budget that resulted in the federal government being shut down twice in 1995 and in early 1996?
   A. The seventy-three first-term Republicans
   B. The Democratic president
   C. The Republican Congress
   D. Both A and C

2. Which of the following has been a factor in creating "gridlock" in Congress, thus inhibiting Congress from acting?
   A. A divided government
   B. A Democrat-controlled Congress facing a Democrat in the White House
   C. A Republican-controlled Congress facing a Republican in the White House
   D. Interference by the Supreme Court

3. Which of the following statements correctly describes Congress' role in national policymaking?
   A. Only the president makes national policy.
   B. Congress has nonlegislative as well as legislative functions.
   C. Congress and the president make national policy.
   D. Both B and C.

4. Congress plays a key role in _____
   A. the legislative process but not in overseeing the operations of independent agencies.
   B. conflict resolution and the legislative process.
   C. overseeing the operations of the independent agencies but not in conflict resolution.
   D. both A and B.

5. Which of the following powers belong to the president?
   A. Giving an annual State of the Union address
   B. Veto power
   C. Power to impound funds appropriated by Congress
   D. All of the above

6. One of the biggest battles in 1997 between Congress and President Clinton was over _____
   A. how to balance the budget.
   B. trade with Eastern Europe.
   C. the question of negotiations with Iran.
   D. where to build the Clinton Presidential Library.

7. The House Republicans wanted to balance the budget by changing the Constitution, but President Clinton and many Democrats feared a constitutional change would _____
   A. encourage an onslaught of constitutional changes.
   B. diminish their chances of winning a majority in 1998.
   C. prevent compromise on most congressional issues.
   D. limit Congress from borrowing money in a time of crisis.

8. The government was shut down twice during 1995–96 for the same reason: Republicans in Congress favored their version of a balanced budget which the president opposed, and twice the president _____
   A. ignored the Republican-backed budget bill.
   B. vetoed the Republican-backed budget bill.
   C. called a press conference to deride the Republicans.
   D. closed the White House to the public.

9. Legislation that calls for the president to notify Congress when he deploys combat troops is called the _____
   A. Budget Impoundment and Control Act.
   B. Military Weapons Buildup Act.
   C. War Powers Act.
   D. Presidential Disclosure Act.

10. In 1990, President George Bush, sending half a million troops into the Persian Gulf to force Hussein to withdraw from Kuwait, used his power as _____
    A. chief negotiator.
    B. commander in chief.
    C. chief executive.
    D. supreme treaty analyst.

ESSAY/PROBLEM QUESTIONS

11. List and discuss two nonlegislative functions of Congress in the policymaking process.

12. Discuss how presidential and congressional legislative powers overlap. Use two examples to illustrate incidents in which these shared powers have led to conflict between the president and the Congress.

13. Every president since Richard Nixon has claimed that the War Powers Act is unconstitutional. Do you believe that this act is unconstitutional and limits presidential power? Why/Why not?

14. Would you support or oppose a balanced budget amendment? Why/Why not?

15. In the 1995–96 government shutdown, whose side would you have supported, President Clinton or congressional Republicans? Why?

ANSWER KEY

The following provides the answers and references for the Practice Test questions. Objectives are referenced using the following abbreviations:
T=Textbook Objectives   V=Video Objectives

1. D .... T1 .... Cummings, p. 374
2. A .... T1 .... Cummings, p. 376
3. D .... T2 .... Cummings, p. 377
4. B .... T2 .... Cummings, pp. 377–379
5. D .... T3 .... Cummings, pp. 424–427
6. A .... V5 .... Video
7. D .... V5 .... Video
8. B .... V6 .... Video
9. C .... V7 .... Video
10. B .... V7 .... Video
11. .... T2 .... Cummings, pp. 377–379
12. .... T2, T3, T4, V6, V7 .... Cummings, pp. 373–375, pp. 424–427, Video
13. .... V7 .... Video
14. .... V5 .... Video
15. .... V6 .... Video

Lesson 17

The Presidency

LESSON ASSIGNMENTS

Review the following assignments in order to schedule your time appropriately. Pay careful attention. The titles and numbers of the textbook chapter, the telecourse guide lesson, and the video program may be different from one another.

Text:
> Cummings and Wise, *Democracy Under Pressure*, Chapter 13, "The President," pp. 407–453.

Video:
> "The Presidency" from the series *Voices in Democracy: United States Government*.

Activities:
> One or more activities may be assigned to this lesson. Refer to your syllabus.

OVERVIEW

This lesson examines the office of the presidency and its role in our system of government. The president's constitutional and extraconstitutional powers are studied, particularly in regard to the question of whether the president has sufficient or excessive power. We examine the roles that the president is called upon to fulfill. The president's ability to fulfill these expectations are studied in light of circumstances that may limit the president's power. In addition to assessing the impact of formal and informal powers on presidential performance, the impact of presidential personality and management style is also evaluated. And of course, the impact and role of other executive actors are explored: the vice presidency, the cabinet, and the White House staff.

LESSON GOAL

Analyze the effect of how presidential management style influences the structure and power of the office, and discuss how the relationship between the president, vice president, cabinet, and White House staff can affect policy.

TEXTBOOK OBJECTIVES

The following objectives are designed to help you get the most from the text. Review them before reading the assignment. You may want to write notes to reinforce what you have learned.

1. Describe the constitutional powers of the U.S. presidency and the congressional checks on the presidency, and discuss the resulting paradox of power.

2. Discuss the events that have increased or decreased presidential power in this century.

3. Identify and discuss the seven key roles the president plays.

4. Assess the contemporary burdens of the president and evaluate the possibility of any president fulfilling these expectations.

5. Explain the relationship of the president with the cabinet and White House staff. Analyze how these organizations help and hinder the president's ability to fulfill presidential duties.

6. Describe the role of the vice president and describe how former vice presidents have felt about the office.

7. Examine the president's informal powers and evaluate their effectiveness.

8. State the constitutional provisions for impeachment and presidential succession, and describe how these procedures have been used in the past.

9. Discuss how presidential character and style affect the president's performance in office.

10. Examine the impact of Watergate and Vietnam on the U.S. presidency and its relationship with Congress.

VIDEO OBJECTIVES

The following objectives are designed to help you get the most from the video segment of this lesson. Review them before watching the video. You may want to write notes to reinforce what you have learned.

11. Describe the qualities which help to determine who is a great president historically. Discuss the greatest presidents according to Professor Schlesinger.

12. Compare and contrast Presidents Carter and Reagan according to Schlesinger's determination of their positions among the historical greats.

13. Explain how a president's personality and management style may affect his or her successes in policy.

14. Compare and contrast the management styles of Presidents Reagan and Carter.

15. Describe the management style of President Bill Clinton and his political leadership successes and failures.

16. Discuss how future presidencies may be evaluated.

PRACTICE TEST

After reading the assignment, watching the video, and addressing the objectives, you should be able to complete the following Practice Test. Some essay questions in this Practice Test may be included in your exams. When you have completed the Practice Test, turn to the Answer Key to score your answers.

MULTIPLE CHOICE

Select the single best answer. If more than one answer is required, it will be so indicated.

1. Under the Constitution, as interpreted by the Supreme Court, which of the following institutions has the primary responsibility for conducting foreign affairs?
   A. Congress
   B. The Senate
   C. The president
   D. Congress and the Supreme Court

2. Which of the following will have a major effect on presidential power?
   A. The times and circumstances in which that power is being exercised
   B. The policy area involved
   C. The situation in which that power is being exercised
   D. All of the above

3. Which of the following diminished presidential power?
   A. Vietnam
   B. Watergate
   C. The Iran-contra affair
   D. All of the above

4. Which of the following contributed to diminishing the powers of today's chief executive?
   A. Foreign affairs
   B. Congress's constitutional power to declare war
   C. The nuclear age and the end of the Cold War
   D. None of the above

5. When Gerald Ford pardoned Richard Nixon for acts that might have been illegal under the laws of the United States, he was performing which presidential role?
   A. Commander in chief
   B. Chief executive
   C. Chief of state
   D. None of the above

6. The president has the sole power to do which of the following when performing in the role of chief diplomat?
   A. Negotiate treaties
   B. Recognize or not recognize a foreign government
   C. Sign executive agreements and put them into effect
   D. All of the above

7. To the role of popular leader, the president normally brings an ideology and a philosophy. Which of the following is identified with limited government?
   A. Franklin D. Roosevelt
   B. Lyndon B. Johnson
   C. John F. Kennedy
   D. Ronald Reagan

8. Which of the following functions is true of the White House chief of staff?
   A. Guards the president's time
   B. Serves as a link with Congress and the executive departments
   C. Advises the president on political affairs and deals with the press
   D. All of the above

9. Which of the following organizations is a part of the Executive Office of the President, which consists of six key agencies and serves the president directly?
   A. The National Security Council
   B. The Office of Management and Budget
   C. The Council of Economic Advisers
   D. All of the above

10. Which vice president succeeded to the presidency in the twentieth century?
    A. Harry Truman
    B. Lyndon Johnson
    C. George Bush
    D. All of the above

11. This first lady of the United States was subpoenaed in January 1996 to answer questions about Whitewater before a federal grand jury.
    A. Nancy Reagan
    B. Hillary Rodham Clinton
    C. Barbara Bush
    D. Rosalynn Carter

12. Which of the following is correct concerning the Nixon-Agnew administration's relationship with the press?
    A. It would accept only written questions from the press.
    B. It instituted "live" unedited TV news conferences.
    C. To an extent that exceeded any modern predecessors, it considered the press a political target.
    D. It limited appearances for the press to "photo opportunities."

13. Which of these statements is correct concerning the effect that the Watergate burglary had on Richard Nixon?
    A. He was subsequently impeached by the House of Representatives but found innocent in the Senate.
    B. He was subsequently impeached by the House of Representatives and found guilty by a two-thirds vote in the Senate.
    C. The House Judiciary Committee recommended that articles of impeachment be voted against him but failed to convince a majority of the whole House to adopt its recommendation.
    D. The House Judiciary Committee recommended that articles of impeachment be voted against him, but he resigned from office before the whole House voted on that recommendation.

14. If there is a disagreement between the president and the vice president as to whether or not the president is disabled or otherwise unable to carry out the duties of the office, which of the following makes the final determination?
    A. The Senate
    B. The Supreme Court
    C. The House of Representatives
    D. Congress

15. If a president follows a policy of doing anything that the needs of the nation demand unless those actions are forbidden by the Constitution, that person follows _____
    A. the classic restrictive view of presidential power.
    B. the stewardship theory of presidential power.
    C. the literalist view of presidential power.
    D. none of the above.

16. A place in history for any president is determined by a complex set of factors; which of the following factors is NOT considered?
    A. Personality and public persuasion
    B. Skill at using presidential powers
    C. Personal debt level
    D. To some extent, fate

17. Together, personality and _____ can be helpful in examining a president's success.
    A. image
    B. media profile
    C. management style
    D. friends

18. Many observers say that President _____ wanted to make all the decisions; whereas, President _____ delegated much of the decision making to his top staff members.
    A. Kennedy/Johnson
    B. Nixon/Ford
    C. Johnson/Bush
    D. Carter/Reagan

19. President Reagan sought advice from wealthy friends who followed him to Washington whom he called his _____
    A. "western cabinet."
    B. "parlor cabinet."
    C. "kitchen cabinet."
    D. "friendly cabinet."

20. More than any other president before him, President Clinton used his _____
    A. veto power.
    B. persuasive powers.
    C. secretary of state.
    D. vice president.

21. President Clinton's self-described legacy is the president who _____
    A. brought respect back to the office.
    B. expanded the power of the office.
    C. built a bridge to the twenty-first century.
    D. ushered in the twenty-first century.

ESSAY/PROBLEM QUESTIONS

22. Discuss this statement: "The American presidency is a place of paradox. It is an office of enormous contrasts, of great power—and great limits." Use the presidencies of Lyndon Johnson, Richard Nixon, and Ronald Reagan as examples of this paradox. Which issue seems to cause presidents the most problems?

23. List three constitutional roles that Cummings and Wise argue a president must perform. Give an example of a presidential action that represents each of the roles listed. Identify a nonconstitutional role that a president must perform. Give an example of a presidential action that illustrates this role.

24. Describe the impeachment process and identify the roles played by the key actors in the process. Use the examples of Nixon's and Clinton's impeachments to illustrate this process.

25. If you were Arthur Schlesinger, III, and you were ranking the presidents from Richard Nixon through Bill Clinton, in what order would you place each one, and why?

26. What management style do you think is most effective for the presidency? Why? Which president do you think has used this style most effectively?

27. Describe the strengths and challenges that Bill Clinton experienced during his presidency.

28. Imagine that you are the president elected in 2048. Describe the skills you will need and the management style you will use. How do you think your term will differ from President Bill Clinton's?

ANSWER KEY

The following provides the answers and references for the Practice Test questions. Objectives are referenced using the following abbreviations:

T=Textbook Objectives   V=Video Objectives

1.	C	T1	Cummings, p. 415
2.	D	T1, T4	Cummings, pp. 448–449
3.	D	T1, T10	Cummings, pp. 409–410
4.	D	T2	Cummings, pp. 414–415
5.	B	T3	Cummings, p. 420
6.	D	T3	Cummings, p. 422
7.	D	T3	Cummings, p. 428
8.	D	T5	Cummings, pp. 431–432
9.	D	T5	Cummings, pp. 433–436
10.	D	T6	Cummings, p. 436
11.	B	T7	Cummings, p. 437
12.	C	T7	Cummings, p. 439
13.	D	T8	Cummings, pp. 441–442
14.	D	T8	Cummings, pp. 445–446
15.	B	T9	Cummings, p. 446
16.	C	V11	Video
17.	C	V13	Video
18.	D	V14	Video
19.	C	V14	Video
20.	D	V15	Video
21.	C	V16	Video
22.		T1, T2, T4, T9, T10	Cummings, pp. 408–429
23.		T3	Cummings, pp. 415–427
24.		T8, T10	Cummings, pp. 440–446
25.		V11, V12, V15	Video
26.		V13, V14, V15	Video
27.		V15	Video
28.		V15, V16	Video

Lesson 17—The Presidency

Lesson 18

Bureaucracy

LESSON ASSIGNMENTS

Review the following assignments in order to schedule your time appropriately. Pay careful attention. The titles and numbers of the textbook chapter, the telecourse guide lesson, and the video program may be different from one another.

Text:
> Cummings and Wise, *Democracy Under Pressure*, Chapter 14, "The Bureaucracy," pp. 455–487.

Video:
> "Bureaucracy" from the series, *Voices in Democracy: United States Government*.

Activities:
> One or more activities may be assigned to this lesson. Refer to your syllabus.

OVERVIEW

This lesson examines the role the bureaucracy plays in American governance and politics. While many Americans may express negative attitudes toward bureaucratic red tape and the large size of the American bureaucracy, most Americans rely on some form of bureaucratic service. The great discretion and independence that bureaucrats enjoy in making their decisions enhances their influence in American politics. However, numerous players interact with bureaucrats and may influence to some degree the rules and regulations they produce. These players include client groups, subgovernments, issue networks, Congress, the president, and the public at large. Over time, Congress and the president have passed a series of reforms that have sought to improve the quality of bureaucratic employees and to increase the efficiency of the bureaucracy. Other forces, such as the courts and bureaucratic "whistle-blowers" have served as checks on bureaucratic power. Historically bureaucratic agencies have substantially regulated multiple aspects of American life and business. Some Americans argue that industry is overregulated. And in certain industries, such as the airline and trucking industries, there has been a movement toward deregulation. The debate continues over whether the federal bureaucracy is too large and whether we are overregulated by the federal government.

LESSON GOAL

Explain the role that a bureaucracy plays in the political process, describe the checks and balances system within the federal bureaucracy, and identify the difficulties in reforming and reducing the size of the bureaucracy.

TEXTBOOK OBJECTIVES

The following objectives are designed to help you get the most from the text. Review them before reading the assignment. You may want to write notes to reinforce what you have learned.

1. Explain the role of bureaucrats, particularly in light of their wide discretionary powers, in shaping public policy.

2. Explain the influence of client groups, Congress, subgovernments (iron triangles), and issue networks on the bureaucratic policy process.

3. Analyze the ability of the president to control the bureaucracy.

4. Identify the differences among the three major executive branch agencies: cabinet departments, executive agencies, and independent regulatory commissions. Identify examples of each.

5. Analyze the ability of independent regulatory agencies to regulate industry, and discuss the recent trend toward deregulation of certain major industries such as trucking and airlines.

6. Discuss the origins of the "spoils system," the fight for civil service reform in the 1880s, and more recent efforts to make the bureaucrats more competent and efficient workers.

7. Discuss the role whistle-blowers and the courts play as checks on bureaucratic power.

8. Analyze the pros and cons of reducing the size of bureaucracy and government regulation. Evaluate how likely it is that efforts at reduction would succeed. Assess the barriers that would make reform difficult and the tools that might make reform easier.

VIDEO OBJECTIVES

The following objectives are designed to help you get the most from the video segment of this lesson. Review them before watching the video. You may want to write notes to reinforce what you have learned.

9. Explain the roles that bureaucrats play in the political process.

10. Describe the checks and balances system which helps to influence the federal bureaucracy.

11. Explain the difficulties in reforming and reducing the size of the bureaucracy.

PRACTICE TEST

After reading the assignment, watching the video, and addressing the objectives, you should be able to complete the following Practice Test. Some essay questions in this Practice Test may be included in your exams. When you have completed the Practice Test, turn to the Answer Key to score your answers.

MULTIPLE CHOICE

Select the single best answer. If more than one answer is required, it will be so indicated.

1. Bureaucrats are said to make policy because _____
   A. they choose among alternative goals and programs.
   B. they participate in the resolution of conflict.
   C. they participate in the initiation of policy proposals.
   D. all of the above.

2. The relationship involving an agency, a committee in Congress, and an industry is commonly called a(n) _____
   A. interrelationship.
   B. multiple corporation.
   C. industrial triangle.
   D. iron triangle.

3. An issue network is _____
   A. a shared knowledge group having to do with some aspect of public policy.
   B. a powerful alliance of mutual benefit among a unit of government, an interest group, and a committee or subcommittee of Congress.
   C. interest groups that are either directly regulated by the bureaucracy or vitally affected by its decisions.
   D. all of the above.

4. The creation of the Office of Management and Budget provides an important tool of bureaucratic control because _____
   A. it allows Congress to control the budgetary process.
   B. it helps the president to monitor and analyze agency budgets.
   C. it acts as an employment agency for the bureaucracy.
   D. none of the above.

5. Which of the following was an attempt by presidents to gain tighter control over the bureaucracy?
   A. The reorganization of its structure
   B. The creation of the Office of Management and Budget
   C. The use of the budgetary process
   D. All of the above

6. The difference between an independent executive agency and an independent regulatory commission is that _____
   A. executive agency heads are appointed by the president.
   B. heads of regulatory commissions are appointed by the president.
   C. independent regulatory commissions are administratively independent of all three branches of government.
   D. executive agency heads can be fired by the president.

7. Which president is associated with deregulation?
   A. Jimmy Carter.
   B. Ronald Reagan.
   C. Franklin Delano Roosevelt.
   D. both A and B.

8. Those who argue that government has gone too far in its attempt to deregulate point to which of the following industries as a case in point?
   A. Railroads
   B. Airlines
   C. Trucking
   D. Communications

9. The Civil Service Reform Act _____
   A. established the spoils system.
   B. was an attempt to reform the inefficiency and corruption that appeared to result from the spoils system.
   C. established the Senior Executive Service (SES).
   D. was advocated by the "Stalwarts" of the Republican Party.

10. Which of the following have publicly exposed waste or corruption that they have learned about in the course of their duties?
    A. Whistle-blowers
    B. Client groups
    C. Constituencies
    D. Rationalists

11. The government machinery that turns laws into regulations and services that affect virtually every aspect of public life is the _____
    A. government corporation.
    B. service agency.
    C. bureaucracy.
    D. regulator.

12. The Health Care Financing Administration is part of an even larger federal bureaucracy, the _____
    A. Health, Education, and Welfare Administration.
    B. American Medical Association.
    C. Health and Human Services Department.
    D. Human Resources Administration.

13. Many presidents have learned that reforming the bureaucracy _____
    A. is easily accomplished.
    B. is no easy road.
    C. takes a national referendum.
    D. requires a ruling from the U.S. Attorney General.

14. One of the national government's biggest spenders has been the _____
    A. Department of Defense.
    B. Department of Justice.
    C. Department of Education.
    D. Department of the Interior.

ESSAY/PROBLEM QUESTIONS

15. Describe the origins of the spoils system and the events that led to its demise. Describe the ways in which the Civil Service Reform Act of 1883 reformed the system of hiring federal employees.

16. Compare and contrast iron triangles and issue networks. Evaluate the power of the president to control the influence of these two forces.

17. Describe three checks on the power of the bureaucracy. Evaluate how likely it is that reform efforts to reduce the bureaucracy would succeed. How might they hinder these reform efforts?

18. If you were an incoming president who had promised to reduce the size of the federal bureaucracy, how would you go about accomplishing this?

19. Describe the federal agencies that you depend on in your daily life and why it is important that they are efficient. Use the Federal Aviation Agency (FAA) as one example and add one other agency that is important to your life.

ANSWER KEY

The following provides the answers and references for the Practice Test questions. Objectives are referenced using the following abbreviations:

T=Textbook Objectives   V=Video Objectives

1. D.............T1..Cummings, p. 462
2. D.............T2, V10...Cummings, p. 464, Video
3. A.............T2..Cummings, p. 464
4. B.............T2..Cummings, p. 466
5. D.............T3..Cummings, p. 466
6. C.............T4..Cummings, p. 474
7. D.............T5..Cummings, pp. 475–476
8. B.............T5..Cummings, p. 476
9. B.............T6..Cummings, pp. 478–479
10. A.............T7..Cummings, p. 480
11. C.............V9..Video
12. C.............V9..Video
13. B.............V11...Video
14. A.............V11...Video
15. ....T6..Cummings, pp. 477–479
16. ....T2, T3..Cummings, p. 464
17. ....T2, T3, T8...Cummings, pp. 482–485
18. ....V9..Video
19. ....V9, V10...Video

Lesson 19

Domestic Policy

LESSON ASSIGNMENTS

Review the following assignments in order to schedule your time appropriately. Pay careful attention. The titles and numbers of the textbook chapter, the telecourse guide lesson, and the video program may be different from one another.

Text:

Cummings and Wise, *Democracy Under Pressure,* Chapter 17, "Government and the Economy," pp. 579–601, and Chapter 18, " Promoting the General Welfare," pp. 603–638.

Video:

"Domestic Policy" from the series *Voices in Democracy: United States Government*.

Activities:

One or more activities may be assigned to this lesson. Refer to your syllabus.

OVERVIEW

In this lesson, we will focus on U.S. domestic policy, including economic policy and general welfare issues. The U.S. system and its economic policies are placed within the context of economic theories. Fiscal and monetary policies are distinguished and are illustrated with examples of U.S. policy. U.S. spending policies are analyzed, particularly trends in deficit spending and the national debt. U.S. trade policy is discussed by identifying the key components of trade policy and by tracing the development of U.S. trade agreements. The area of domestic policy that deals with general welfare issues includes government regulation of business and labor and consumer protection. This lesson traces the development of (1) key social insurance programs such as Social Security, unemployment insurance, and Medicare and (2) key public assistance such as the former AFDC and Medicaid. Then the effectiveness of these programs is evaluated. Finally, the role of government in education and environmental policy is discussed. Ultimately, this lesson should provide you with the information you would need to evaluate the appropriate role of government in this broad policy area and to evaluate the effectiveness of these programs and their place in future U.S. policy.

LESSON GOAL

You should be able to explain the factors and influences that shape domestic policy and the policy's impact on people in the United States.

TEXTBOOK OBJECTIVES

The following objectives are designed to help you get the most from the text. Review them before reading the assignment. You may want to write notes to reinforce what you have learned.

1. Identify and describe the main theories of economic policy. Be able to distinguish between fiscal and monetary policy. Illustrate with contemporary and historical examples.

2. Describe the powers and tools used by the federal government in fiscal and monetary policy. Illustrate with contemporary examples and identify the primary factors involved.

3. Describe and evaluate recent U.S. spending and borrowing policies. Illustrate with examples from contemporary budget battles.

4. Discuss the components and key concerns of U.S. international trade policy using contemporary examples to illustrate.

5. Assess the economy of the 1990s and evaluate the role that the government should play in regulating the economy.

6. Describe the key goals of government regulation of business and labor. Illustrate with historical and contemporary examples of government regulation.

7. Identify and discuss the principal protections the government has provided consumers.

8. Trace the development of (1) social insurance programs, such as Social Security, Medicare, and unemployment insurance and (2) public assistance programs, such as the former AFDC and Medicaid. Describe the components of each program and identify the differences between the types of programs. Evaluate the effectiveness and appropriateness of these programs.

9. Discuss the role of the federal government in education policy.

10. Discuss the role of the federal government in the key areas of environmental policy, illustrating with contemporary examples. Evaluate the effectiveness and appropriateness of these programs.

VIDEO OBJECTIVES

The following objectives are designed to help you get the most from the video segment of this lesson. Review them before watching the video. You may want to write notes to reinforce what you have learned.

11. Explain some of the factors and influences that shape domestic policy and its impact on individuals in the United States, focusing on the Freedom to Farm Act of 1996.

12. Explain the pros and cons of U.S. labor policy and its effect on domestic policy.

13. Identify the potential conflicts between groups involved in shaping domestic policy.

PRACTICE TEST

After reading the assignment, watching the video, and addressing the objectives, you should be able to complete the following Practice Test. Some essay questions in this Practice Test may be included in your exams. When you have completed the Practice Test, turn to the Answer Key to score your answers.

MULTIPLE CHOICE

Select the single best answer. If more than one answer is required, it will be so indicated.

1. Which of the following statements accurately describes *laissez-faire* economics?
   A. The principles are associated with Milton Friedman.
   B. The theory argues for deficit spending during recessions.
   C. The theory argues for a "hands-off" economic policy.
   D. The theory argues for strong government intervention in the marketplace.

2. One result of the Reagan program was that _____
   A. the wealthiest 5 percent of Americans received a massive tax hike.
   B. many social services were cut.
   C. the budget was balanced.
   D. defense spending was cut.

3. Which of the following steps must be taken before federal funds may be spent?
   A. A budget resolution is passed to set overall spending targets.
   B. An authorization to spend federal money is adopted.
   C. An appropriations bill is passed to pay for the spending that has been authorized.
   D. All of the above.

4. Which of the following is responsible for controlling the supply of money and the cost and availability of credit?
   A. Congress
   B. General Accounting Office
   C. Office of Management and Budget
   D. Federal Reserve Board

5. A budget deficit is _____
   A. the gap between government's income and outlays.
   B. the total amount of money that the United States owes to its debtors.
   C. a rarely occurring phenomenon in recent years.
   D. both B and C.

6. A federal tax on imports is _____
   A. a GATT.
   B. an oligopoly.
   C. a tariff.
   D. a court injunction.

7. Which of the following statements correctly describes NAFTA?
   A. It is a trade agreement between Mexico, Canada, and the United States.
   B. Labor bitterly opposed the agreement.
   C. Business generally supported the agreement.
   D. All of the above.

8. The aim of the Sherman Antitrust Act was to _____
   A. encourage competition in business and prevent the growth of monopolies.
   B. create the National Labor Relations Board.
   C. prohibit closed shops.
   D. prohibit employers from discriminating against workers for union activity or membership.

9. Charging that the computer software giant was using its monopoly in personal computer operating systems to gain competitive advantage in other software fields, such as Internet browsers, in 1998 the Justice Department filed an antitrust suit against _____
   A. IBM.
   B. Alcatel.
   C. Microsoft.
   D. EDS.

10. A multi-interest, and often multinational, corporation that may, under one roof, manufacture products ranging from missiles to baby bottles is _____
    A. a monopoly.
    B. an oligopoly.
    C. a conglomerate.
    D. a closed shop.

11. In order to promote the general welfare, the federal government fills which of the following roles?
    A. Regulator
    B. Promoter
    C. Protector
    D. All of the above

12. A crusader for auto safety who brought federal legislation to bear and who prodded the automobile industry to produce safer cars and to recall those with suspected defects was _____
    A. George Bush.
    B. Bill Clinton.
    C. Ross Perot.
    D. Ralph Nader.

13. What do the Auto Safety Law, the Truth-in-Packaging Law, and the Meat and Poultry Inspection Law have in common?
    A. They were vetoed by Republican presidents.
    B. They are among the principal federal consumer laws.
    C. They were part of Franklin Delano Roosevelt's New Deal program.
    D. They have nothing in common.

14. The Social Security Act and amendments to it provide for _____
    A. disability insurance.
    B. old-age and survivors insurance.
    C. Medicare.
    D. all of the above.

15. The federal law that established federally insured loans for college students and established the work-study programs was known as _____
    A. the Morrill Act.
    B. the Higher Education Act of 1965 (Pell grants).
    C. the National Defense Education Act.
    D. all of the above.

16. The controversy surrounding the northern spotted owl illustrates which of the following?
    A. The controversy over federal support of bird watching
    B. The problems that states have in protecting migratory birds from being killed
    C. The controversy over which species qualify for protection on the endangered species list
    D. The controversy that may develop when environmental concerns affect employment

17. The controversial secretary of the interior in the Reagan administration who seemed to favor development over environmental concerns was _____
    A. Edwin Meese III.
    B. Margaret Heckler.
    C. James Watt.
    D. Milton Friedman.

18. Where did a potential nuclear disaster take place in the United States?
    A. Chernobyl
    B. Three Mile Island, Pennsylvania
    C. San Luis Obispo, California
    D. Sherbrooke, Maine

19. After more than half a century of government quotas and controls, the U.S. farmers themselves can decide what to grow, due to _____
    A. strong farmer union membership.
    B. reduction in the amount of farming regulations.
    C. a major overhaul in domestic farm policy.
    D. new farming techniques.

20. The legislation designed to move U.S. agriculture from government dependence toward a free-market approach is known as the 1996 _____
    A. Farmers Relief Act.
    B. Farmers Free-Market Act.
    C. Freedom for Agriculture Act.
    D. Freedom to Farm Act.

21. The nation's farm policy used to protect farmers through a program of government _____
    A. subsidies that fluctuated with market prices.
    B. subsidies that stabilized market prices.
    C. give-aways that caused increased market prices.
    D. give-aways that resulted in decreased market prices.

22. By invoking a seventy-year-old statute called the Railway Labor Act, President Clinton intervened because a strike threatened _____
    A. the railroad industry.
    B. interstate commerce.
    C. international trade.
    D. labor relations.

23. The largest labor union in the United States is the _____
    A. Labor Negotiators Union.
    B. Union of Workers and Employers.
    C. NAACP.
    D. AFL-CIO.

24. The U.S. fishing industry has lost a billion dollars and tens of thousands of jobs because of _____ by other countries and by United States fishers.
    A. catching the breeding fish
    B. destroying the natural habitats
    C. overharvesting
    D. underharvesting

ESSAY/PROBLEM QUESTIONS

25. Describe the different theories concerning the role of the government in the economy. How would you describe the U.S. economic system? What role do you think the U.S. government should play in the economy in the future? Why?

26. Define *deficit* and *national debt*. Explain how the two concepts are related. Describe the recent trends relating to these two phenomena and explain how Congress has attempted to deal with them. Evaluate whether these efforts have been successful and the odds for success in the future.

27. Define *social insurance*, *public assistance*, and *entitlements*. Be sure to distinguish the differences between the three concepts and give examples to illustrate each.

28. Compare the provisions for farmers in New Deal policies and in the Freedom to Farm Act.

29. Explain the ramifications of an airline's threat to strike and the UPS strike on domestic policy.

30. What problems might arise between one group that wants to develop policy to safeguard and improve its means of making a living and another group that attempts to protect the environment? Also explain the conflicts which have arisen between fishers in Canada and the United States due to the Pacific Salmon Treaty.

ANSWER KEY

The following provides the answers and references for the Practice Test questions. Objectives are referenced using the following abbreviations:

T=Textbook Objectives   V=Video Objectives

1.	C	T1	Cummings, p. 584
2.	B	T1	Cummings, p. 585
3.	D	T2	Cummings, p. 586
4.	D	T2	Cummings, p. 590
5.	A	T3	Cummings, p. 586
6.	C	T4	Cummings, p. 594
7.	D	T4	Cummings, p. 594
8.	A	T6	Cummings, p. 607
9.	C	T6	Cummings, p. 607
10.	C	T6	Cummings, p. 608
11.	D	T6, T8	Cummings, p. 605
12.	D	T7	Cummings, p. 613
13.	B	T7	Cummings, p. 614
14.	D	T8	Cummings, pp. 615–616
15.	B	T9	Cummings, p. 623
16.	D	T10	Cummings, pp. 625–626
17.	C	T10	Cummings, p. 628
18.	B	T10	Cummings, p. 633
19.	C	V11	Video
20.	D	V11	Video
21.	A	V11	Video
22.	B	V12	Video
23.	D	V12	Video
24.	C	V13	Video
25.		T1, T5	Cummings, pp. 584–586
26.		T3	Cummings, pp. 586–590
27.		T8	Cummings, pp. 614–619
28.		V11	Video
29.		V12	Video
30.		V13	Video

Lesson 20

Foreign Policy

LESSON ASSIGNMENTS

Review the following assignments in order to schedule your time appropriately. Pay careful attention. The titles and numbers of the textbook chapter, the telecourse guide lesson, and the video program may be different from one another.

Text:
> Cummings and Wise, *Democracy Under Pressure*, Chapter 16, "Foreign Policy and National Security," pp. 533–558 and pp. 561–569.

Video:
> "Foreign Policy" from the series *Voices in Democracy: United States Government*.

Activities:
> One or more activities may be assigned to this lesson. Refer to your syllabus.

OVERVIEW

This lesson examines the key actors and issues in U.S. foreign policy. The development of U.S. foreign policy over time is traced, highlighting the dominant foreign policy issues and themes. We examine the delineation of the power to conduct foreign policy and the cooperation and conflict between the president and Congress in using these powers. Other key actors and institutions are identified and their roles in the process are evaluated. Additionally, the impact of the American public and political parties on foreign policy is explored. This lesson also discusses the defense establishment and traces the development of its policy on strategic arms.

Because of the end of the Cold War between the Soviet Union and the United States, foreign policy strategies are evolving. The North Atlantic Treaty

Organization (NATO) is examined as it does or does not meet the needs of our foreign policy. New coalitions have formed to deal with crises such as the Gulf War and the world's concern about Iraq's weapons of mass destruction.

LESSON GOAL

Describe the roles of the president, his or her advisors, and Congress in influencing the decision making of foreign policy and explain the power of organized citizen groups in affecting it.

TEXTBOOK OBJECTIVES

The following objectives are designed to help you get the most from the text. Review them, then read the assignment. You may want to write notes to reinforce what you have learned.

1. Describe the dramatic changes in foreign affairs that occurred in the late 1980s and early 1990s. Describe the key foreign policy concerns of the 1990s.

2. Identify and discuss the key issues of contemporary foreign policy and the competing viewpoints on these issues. Discuss the issues relevant to the following periods of U.S. foreign policy: isolationism, the Cold War and containment, Vietnam, détente, post-Vietnam, post–Cold War.

3. Describe and evaluate the president's powers and constraints in conducting foreign policy.

4. Describe and evaluate the role that Congress plays in conducting foreign policy.

5. Identify and discuss other key factors and institutions in U.S. foreign policy and their role in this process.

6. Describe the role the public plays in foreign policy.

7. Describe the ways in which political parties affect foreign policy.

8. Identify and describe the key components of the defense establishment. Discuss their functions in foreign policymaking.

9. Identify the key issues and strategies in U.S. strategic arms policy.

VIDEO OBJECTIVES

The following objectives are designed to help you get the most from the video segment of this lesson. Review them, then watch the video. You may want to write notes to reinforce what you have learned.

10. Describe the development and demise of the Cold War.

11. Using the Persian Gulf War as an example, explain the post–Cold War shift in U.S. foreign policy that includes effective use of U.S. intelligence and a military coalition.

12. Describe the changes in NATO and European partnerships following the Cold War.

13. Explain the power of organized citizen groups in affecting foreign policy.

PRACTICE TEST

After reading the assignment, watching the video, and addressing the objectives, you should be able to complete the following Practice Test. Some essay questions in this Practice Test may be included in your exams. When you have completed the Practice Test, turn to the Answer Key to score your answers.

MULTIPLE CHOICE

Select the single best answer. If more than one answer is required, it will be so indicated.

1. With the end of the Cold War, the Clinton administration based its foreign policy on which of the following principles?
    A. A policy of containment
    B. A zero-sum game
    C. Revising the Truman doctrine
    D. A policy of democratic "enlargement"

2. The sum of the goals, decisions, and actions that govern a nation's relations with the rest of the world is _____
   A. domestic policy.
   B. politics.
   C. foreign policy.
   D. political culture.

3. By deciding to join the United Nations after World War II, the United States was adopting which form of foreign policy?
   A. Balance of power
   B. Interventionist
   C. Isolationist
   D. Internationalist

4. The Truman Doctrine was based on which of the following foreign policy options?
   A. Isolationism
   B. Containment
   C. "Back to normalcy"
   D. "Gunboat diplomacy"

5. In conducting foreign policy, the president plays which of the following roles?
   A. Commander in chief
   B. Chief diplomat
   C. Chief executive
   D. Both A and B

6. Which of the following is a constitutional power of Congress?
   A. To declare war
   B. To appropriate money for defense
   C. To raise and support armies
   D. All of the above

7. Which of the following was created to advise the president on the integration of domestic, foreign, and military policies relating to national security?
   A. The National Security Council
   B. The State Department
   C. The Pentagon
   D. All of the above

8. John Poindexter and Oliver North were _____
   A. secretaries of state.
   B. national security advisers.
   C. members of the National Security Council staff who were involved in the Iran-contra scandal.
   D. directors of the CIA under Ronald Reagan.

9. The CIA director is responsible for coordinating activities with which other agency?
   A. The Defense Intelligence Agency (DIA)
   B. The FBI
   C. The National Security Agency (NSA)
   D. All of the above

10. Lyndon Johnson's decision not to seek reelection to the presidency in 1968 illustrates _____
    A. that a president who passes significant domestic legislation is considered to be so successful that there is no incentive to run again.
    B. that intense domestic reaction to foreign policy has a great impact on government and the political fortunes of public officials, including the president.
    C. how the Twenty-second Amendment, which prohibits a person from serving more than two terms as president, works.
    D. that vice presidents who succeed to the presidency due to the death of the president are never able to serve more than one term in that office.

11. Those who argue that "politics stops at the water's edge" are said to be advocates of _____
    A. bipartisanship.
    B. isolationism.
    C. internationalism.
    D. partisanship.

12. Which of the following is true concerning the relationship between foreign policy and defense policy?
    A. Foreign policy and defense policy are intimately linked.
    B. Ideally, foreign policy establishes the broad outlines within which the defense establishment must work.
    C. The president must see that the generals serve the president's foreign policy goals rather than the other way around.
    D. All of the above.

13. The Western world's biggest employer is _____
    A. General Motors.
    B. the secretary of defense of the United States.
    C. IBM.
    D. impossible to determine.

14. Which principle is deeply rooted in the Constitution and in the traditions of the United States?
    A. The secretary of defense must have a military background.
    B. The military establishment should be under civilian control.
    C. The State Department should be under military control.
    D. All of the above.

15. The training of Special Forces in guerrilla warfare and "counterinsurgency" occurred when the United States adopted which of the following defense strategies?
    A. Massive nuclear retaliation
    B. Flexible response
    C. Balance of power
    D. Isolationism

16. At the end of World War II, the world's two remaining "superpowers" were _____
    A. Great Britain and the United States.
    B. the United States and West Germany.
    C. the Soviet Union and NATO.
    D. the Soviet Union and the United States.

17. In January 1991, the U.S. military target was not communist aggression but rather the protection of _____
    A. Middle East oil.
    B. Russian nuclear weapons.
    C. Egypt's Suez Canal.
    D. Saudi Arabia's water supply.

18. The Gulf War demonstrated that the U.S. military could be used in a new way, even _____
    A. with a co-ed military.
    B. in the absence of a communist threat.
    C. in peaceful negotiations.
    D. without congressional approval.

19. In 1998, the North Atlantic Treaty Organization invited three new countries to join the organization; the newly invited countries had once been _____
    A. adversaries, allied with the former Soviet Union.
    B. members of the Allied Forces under General Eisenhower.
    C. allies with Nazi Germany.
    D. known as the hub of the Axis powers.

20. The Clinton Administration had been involved with Ireland by _____
    A. giving a U.S. visa to Gerry Adams, head of Sinn Fein.
    B. mediating an IRA cease-fire.
    C. establishing peace talks and possible agreement.
    D. all of the above.

ESSAY/PROBLEM QUESTIONS

21. Compare the differences in U.S. policy when it embraced isolationism and when it embraced internationalism. How do these opposing viewpoints relate to the question of U.S. foreign policy in the post–Cold War era? Identify presidential candidates that have taken each position.

22. Describe the structure of the defense establishment by indicating the relationships that exist among the offices of president, secretary of defense, the service secretaries, and the Joint Chiefs of Staff. What are the responsibilities of each office in national security? How are each of these actors (with the exception of the president) selected?

23. Describe the ways in which the public can or has affected U.S. foreign policy. It is often claimed that the public is too uninformed on world affairs and therefore should not be able to affect foreign policy. Evaluate this assessment and discuss the validity of this claim in light of democratic principles.

24. What effect did the Persian Gulf War have on the shift in the U.S. foreign policymaking?

25. Explain the major differences in the North Atlantic Treaty Organization (NATO) during the Cold War and after the Cold War. What proposals are made to expand NATO?

26. Explain how the Cuban-American foundation has affected the U.S. foreign policy with Cuba. How do the Canadians view our policy with Cuba? How should the U.S. policies with Cuba be handled with the end of the Cold War?

ANSWER KEY

The following provides the answers and references for the Practice Test questions. Objectives are referenced using the following abbreviations:

T=Textbook Objectives   V=Video Objectives

#	Answer	Objective	Reference
1.	D	T1	Cummings, p. 547
2.	C	T2	Cummings, p. 535
3.	D	T2	Cummings, p. 538
4.	B	T2	Cummings, p. 539
5.	D	T3	Cummings, p. 549
6.	D	T4	Cummings, p. 550
7.	A	T5	Cummings, p. 552
8.	C	T5	Cummings, pp. 552–553
9.	D	T5	Cummings, p. 556
10.	B	T6	Cummings, p. 561
11.	B	T7	Cummings, p. 538
12.	D	T8	Cummings, p. 565
13.	B	T8	Cummings, p. 566
14.	B	T8	Cummings, p. 565
15.	B	T9	Cummings, p. 567
16.	D	V10	Video
17.	A	V11	Video
18.	B	V11	Video
19.	A	V12	Video
20.	D	V13	Video
21.		T1, T2	Cummings, pp. 537–549
22.		T5	Cummings, pp. 563–566
23.		T6	Cummings, pp. 561–562
24.		V11	Video
25.		V12	Video
26.		V13	Video

Lesson 20—Foreign Policy

Lesson 21

Global Politics

LESSON ASSIGNMENTS

Review the following assignments in order to schedule your time appropriately. Pay careful attention. The titles and numbers of the textbook chapter, the telecourse guide lesson, and the video program may be different from one another.

Text:

Cummings and Wise, *Democracy Under Pressure*, Chapter 16, "Foreign Policy and National Security," pp. 547–549 ("The Post–Cold War World"), pp. 552–561 ("The Machinery" and "The United Nations"), pp. 569–570 ("Arms Control and Disarmament"), and pp. 573–574 ("America's World Role in the 21st Century").

Video:

"Global Politics" from the series *Voices in Democracy: United States Government*.

Activities:

One or more activities may be assigned to this lesson. Refer to your syllabus.

OVERVIEW

This lesson examines the participation of the United States in global affairs. It examines the role of key U.S. institutions (such as AID, USIA, the Peace Corps, and the Arms Control and Disarmament Agency) in global affairs and U.S. foreign policy. We describe the membership and main decision-making bodies of the United Nations (UN) and evaluate the function and effectiveness of the UN in world politics. The international efforts to control arms are traced. The function of the UN in the post–Cold War era is analyzed as examples of contemporary issues have emerged such as peacekeeping missions, environmental treaties, and human rights. This lesson illustrates the interconnectedness of U.S. foreign policy with events and institutions around the world. It will enable you to engage in a cursory evaluation of the global situation and contemporary issues that face the nations of the world in the future.

LESSON GOAL

You should be able to describe the basic structure of the United Nations as a forum for problem solving, peacekeeping, and global communications and the interconnectedness of U.S. foreign policy in a global community.

TEXTBOOK OBJECTIVES

The following objectives are designed to help you get the most from the text. Review them before reading the assignment. You may want to write notes to reinforce what you have learned.

1. Discuss U.S. policy in the post–Cold War era, particularly in regard to the revised debate between isolationists and internationalists.

2. Identify and describe the role of the AID, USIA, the Peace Corps, and the Arms Control and Disarmament Agency in U.S. foreign policy.

3. Describe the UN's role in past and contemporary international issues. Evaluate its successes and losses. Evaluate the U.S. relationship with the UN in the past few years.

4. Trace the history of international efforts at arms control and disarmament. Identify and describe the history and components of key treaties.

5. Describe the potential role that may be filled by the United States in the world in the next decade and the next century.

VIDEO OBJECTIVES

The following objectives are designed to help you get the most from the video segment of this lesson. Review them before watching the video. You may want to write notes to reinforce what you have learned.

6. Describe the basic structure of the UN as a forum for problem solving, peacekeeping, and global communications. Evaluate the responsibility of the United States as a very powerful and rich member nation in the UN today and in the future.

7. Explain the United Nations' and the United States' roles by looking at success in Haiti and failure in Somalia.

8. Discuss the global effect of environmental factors and describe how economic interests sometimes collide with those factors. Examine the relationship between countries when they differ on solutions.

9. Explain the struggle between human rights and economic objectives in the global community when cultural differences between countries conflict.

PRACTICE TEST

After reading the assignment, watching the video, and addressing the objectives, you should be able to complete the following Practice Test. Some essay questions in this Practice Test may be included in your exams. When you have completed the Practice Test, turn to the Answer Key to score your answers.

MULTIPLE CHOICE

Select the single best answer. If more than one answer is required, it will be so indicated.

1. Which of the following might be included in a U.S. mission in a foreign capital?
   A. Military attachés
   B. Agents of the CIA
   C. Representatives of the United States Information Agency (USIA)
   D. All of the above

2. In the past, which of the following played an active role in negotiations between the United States and the Soviet Union to reduce the number of nuclear arms in the two countries?
   A. The International Bank for Reconstruction and Development (World Bank)
   B. The United States Information Agency (USIA)
   C. The Agency for International Development (AID)
   D. The Arms Control and Disarmament Agency

3. Besides the United States, which of the following is a permanent member of the UN Security Council and possesses a veto over that organization's policies?
   A. Great Britain
   B. France
   C. The People's Republic of China
   D. All of the above

4. The administration of the UN is the responsibility of the _____
   A. General Assembly.
   B. Security Council.
   C. United Nations Educational, Scientific, and Cultural Organization (UNESCO).
   D. Secretariat.

5. By 2000, the UN had expanded from its original 50 to 189 members. The secretary-general was _____
   A. Madeleine Albright from the United States.
   B. Boutros Boutros-Ghali from Egypt.
   C. Kofi Annan from Ghana.
   D. James Baker from the United States.

6. The first treaty in which the United States and the USSR agreed to reduce their nuclear arsenals was _____
   A. the Strategic Arms Limitation Talks.
   B. the Nuclear Nonproliferation Treaty.
   C. the Intermediate-range Nuclear Forces Treaty.
   D. détente.

7. Which United States president negotiated the START II treaty that was ratified by the Senate in 1996?
   A. Carter
   B. Reagan
   C. Clinton
   D. Bush

8. The two most prominent bodies of the UN are the _____
   A. General Assembly and the Aid to Families Agency.
   B. Security Council and Board of Peacekeepers.
   C. General Assembly and the Security Council.
   D. Board of Peacekeepers and the Security Council

9. The goal of the UN peacekeeping mission in Somalia was to _____
   A. squash gang violence and distribute food.
   B. protect the citizens from communism and treat the injured.
   C. feed the children and establish hospitals.
   D. build schools and hospitals.

10. In 1996, when Secretary of State Warren Christopher visited the Brazilian rain forest, the _____ had become a foreign policy priority.
    A. peace
    B. economy
    C. environment
    D. trade balance

11. Trade issues sometimes interfere with the United States' concern for _____
    A. balancing the budget of the UN.
    B. global human rights.
    C. cultural diversity.
    D. none of the above.

12. Policymakers calculate the global consequences of all of the following situations EXCEPT _____
    A. destroying forests in South America.
    B. punishing countries because of the way they address human rights.
    C. requiring the help of nongovernmental groups in carrying out foreign policy.
    D. all of the above.

ESSAY/PROBLEM QUESTIONS

13. Discuss what role the United States should play in world affairs in the future. Be sure to include a discussion of the proper role of the United States in the UN.

14. Discuss the responsibilities of the AID, USIA, the Peace Corps, and the Arms Control and Disarmament Agency.

15. Describe the responsibilities and the membership of the UN Security Council and the UN General Assembly. Describe the U.S. role in each of these bodies.

16. Explain the goals and functions of the UN. What role does the United States play in the operation of the UN? Explain.

17. Compare and contrast U.S. involvement through the UN in Somalia and in Haiti.

18. Explain the interconnectedness of the global environment relative to global economics on U.S. global politics.

19. What role do you think human rights should play in U.S. foreign policy and in UN global politics?

ANSWER KEY

The following provides the answers and references for the Practice Test questions. Objectives are referenced using the following abbreviations:
T=Textbook Objectives   V=Video Objectives

#	Ans	Obj	Reference
1.	D	T2	Cummings, p. 554
2.	D	T2	Cummings, p. 554
3.	D	T3, V6	Cummings, p. 560, Video
4.	D	T3	Cummings, p. 561
5.	C	T3	Cummings, p. 561
6.	C	T4	Cummings, p. 570
7.	D	T4	Cummings, p. 570
8.	C	V6	Video
9.	A	V7	Video
10.	C	V8	Video
11.	B	V9	Video
12.	D	V9	Video
13.		T1, T5, V6	Cummings, pp. 547–549, pp. 560–561, and pp. 573–574, Video
14.		T2	Cummings, pp. 558–560
15.		T3	Cummings, pp. 560–561
16.		V6	Video
17.		V7	Video
18.		V8	Video
19.		V9	Video

Lesson 22

Federal Courts

LESSON ASSIGNMENTS

Review the following assignments in order to schedule your time appropriately. Pay careful attention. The titles and numbers of the textbook chapter, the telecourse guide lesson, and the video program may be different from one another.

Text:
  Cummings and Wise, *Democracy Under Pressure*, Chapter 15, "Justice" pp. 489–508.

Video:
  "Federal Courts" from the series *Voices in Democracy: United States Government*.

Activities:
  One or more activities may be assigned to this lesson. Refer to your syllabus.

OVERVIEW

This lesson examines the U.S. judiciary system and its role in U.S. politics. First, we trace the development of one of the courts' most significant powers, judicial review, and then evaluate the opposing viewpoints on this power. Next, we examine the three most recent Supreme Court chief justices and the decisions made under their leadership. These courts and their ideological outputs are compared and evaluated. The Rehnquist Court's decisions in *Bush v. Vera* and *Romer v. Evans* are examined to determine the philosophical and political stands of its members. The process of Supreme Court nomination is also examined in both a historical context and more recent nominations. We discuss the ways in which Congress and the president may attempt to limit the Court's influence. Additionally, the Supreme Court's internal processes are described. And finally, the structure and process of the federal and state courts are described and contrasted. Overall, this study provides you with an overview of the judicial process as well as insights that may help you to evaluate the role of the courts in the political process and in U.S. policymaking.

LESSON GOAL

Explain the U.S. Supreme Court as an institution delineated by politics, personalities, and philosophies of individual judges and how the Court affects the concerns and attitudes of the times.

TEXTBOOK OBJECTIVES

The following objectives are designed to help you get the most from the text. Review them before reading the assignment. You may want to write notes to reinforce what you have learned.

1. Explain judicial review and trace its development through *Marbury v. Madison*. Evaluate the opposing viewpoints of judicial review.

2. Describe the three broad areas of decisions during the Warren Court.

3. Describe the key issues and decisions of the Supreme Court during the Burger Court.

4. Describe the key issues and decisions of the Supreme Court during the Rehnquist Court.

5. Describe the process of presidential nomination of Supreme Court justices. Explain the relationship of politics and ideology in the nomination process, and evaluate the ability of the president to predict the behavior of his or her nominees.

6. Explain the ways in which Congress can limit the Supreme Court's influence.

7. Describe the internal processes of the Supreme Court.

8. Describe the basic structure of the federal and state courts. Identify the key types of courts and the areas of law with which they deal.

VIDEO OBJECTIVES

The following objectives are designed to help you get the most from the video segment of this lesson. Review them before watching the video. You may want to write notes to reinforce what you have learned.

9. Describe the conflicted nature of the U.S. Supreme Court over time as it attempts to be judicious but in fact is a political institution.

10. Explain the U.S. Supreme Court as an institution delineated by politics, personalities, and philosophies of individual judges and how the Court affects and reflects the concerns and attitudes of the times.

11. Describe the composition of the current U.S. Supreme Court and the members' philosophical differences which may contribute to and reflect wider political changes taking place in the United States.

12. Discuss the philosophical differences between different members of the U.S. Supreme Court as demonstrated in *Romer v. Evans* and *Bush v. Vera*.

PRACTICE TEST

After reading the assignment, watching the video, and addressing the objectives, you should be able to complete the following Practice Test. Some essay questions in this Practice Test may be included in your exams. When you have completed the Practice Test, turn to the Answer Key to score your answers.

MULTIPLE CHOICE

Select the single best answer. If more than one answer is required, it will be so indicated.

1. The power of the courts to declare acts of Congress, actions of the federal executive, or laws that are enacted by any level of government to be unconstitutional is the power of _____
   A. judicial review.
   B. *certiorari*.
   C. precedent.
   D. *stare decisis*.

2. Which of the following statements correctly describes the Warren Court?
   A. It handed down decisions that called for the end of segregation in public schools.
   B. It handed down decisions that made it more difficult for law enforcement officials to prosecute criminals.
   C. It handed down decisions that banned government-sponsored prayer in schools.
   D. All of the above.

3. Which of the following would be considered a liberal ruling made by the Burger Court?
   A. It legalized abortion.
   B. It declined to stop publication of the Pentagon Papers.
   C. It extended the right of counsel to poor defendants even in misdemeanor cases.
   D. All of the above.

4. Which of the following statements correctly describes the Rehnquist Court?
   A. The Court's conservative bloc was often the dominant force.
   B. On some cases the Court handed down liberal decisions.
   C. It would be hard to apply ideological terms to the Court's decisions.
   D. Both A and B

5. Which of the following statements correctly describes presidential nominations of persons to the Supreme Court?
   A. The Senate has confirmed the vast majority of the presidents' nominations.
   B. The president tends to nominate candidates across both political parties.
   C. Once on the Court, the president's nominees tend to vote the way the president would have predicted.
   D. The confirmation process is rarely political.

6. Under the Constitution, which of the following determines the size of the Supreme Court?
   A. The president
   B. Congress
   C. The Constitution designates the number as nine
   D. The Senate

7. Congress may attempt to overturn specific Supreme Court rulings by utilizing which of the following?
   A. Proposing an amendment to the Constitution
   B. Passing legislation
   C. Withholding the salaries of the Supreme Court justices
   D. Both A and B

8. When the Supreme Court hears a case directly, it is exercising _____
   A. original jurisdiction.
   B. appellate jurisdiction.
   C. *certiorari* jurisdiction.
   D. majority jurisdiction.

9. An opinion assigned by the chief justice when the chief justice votes with the majority of the Court is _____
   A. the majority opinion.
   B. the concurring opinion.
   C. the dissenting opinion.
   D. the consensus opinion.

10. Which of the following is a trial court?
    A. The Supreme Court
    B. Circuit courts
    C. District courts
    D. All of the above

11. All federal judges receive their positions on the bench by an appointment by the _____
    A. president, subject to senate approval.
    B. president, subject to congressional approval.
    C. chief justice, subject to congressional approval.
    D. attorney general, subject to senate approval.

12. Which of the following presidents appointed more African American and women judges?
    A. Reagan
    B. Clinton
    C. Bush
    D. Carter

13. The political environment of the Supreme Court affects decisions in different ways, such as _____
    A. the general social climate of the times.
    B. specific political pressures creating intolerable conflict.
    C. the desire to retreat to very early decisions of the court.
    D. both A and B.

14. After appointment to the bench, which of the following actions is NOT true of Supreme Court justices?
    A. They are largely protected from political obligations.
    B. They may vote however they see fit.
    C. They may receive donations for renomination.
    D. They are not always predictable.

15. The Supreme Court decision in *Bush v. Vera* affected not only the candidates, but also the _____
    A. voters.
    B. contributors.
    C. state legislators.
    D. political party leaders.

16. In *Romer v. Evans*, Justice Kennedy stated that Colorado's Amendment 2 violates the U.S. Constitution's _____
    A. separation of powers clause.
    B. due process clause.
    C. equal protection clause.
    D. civil liberties clause.

ESSAY/PROBLEM QUESTIONS

17. Define *judicial review*. Briefly explain the key facts of the case *Marbury v. Madison*. Explain how Marshall's decision dealt with the Judiciary Act and what justification Marshall gave. Evaluate whether the practice of judicial review fits well within a democratic system of government.

18. Identify and describe the three broad areas of decisions that are identified with the Warren Court. Compare these decisions with those in the following Burger Court.

19. Describe the constitutionally mandated process of Supreme Court nominations. Describe the role of ideological and political concerns in the nomination process. Evaluate whether the political nature of the process is appropriate and whether it fits within the framework of governance envisioned by the original framers of the Constitution.

20. Do you support or oppose the lifetime term of Supreme Court justices? Why? Explain the role of presidential appointments and the president's future influence on decisions of the court.

21. If you were a Supreme Court justice, how would you have voted in *Bush v. Vera*? Explain your decision.

22. What is your reaction to the Supreme Court's decision in Colorado's case of *Romer v. Evans*? Explain your reaction.

ANSWER KEY

The following provides the answers and references for the Practice Test questions. Objectives are referenced using the following abbreviations:

T=Textbook Objectives   V=Video Objectives

#	Ans	Obj	Reference
1.	A	T1	Cummings, p. 495
2.	D	T2	Cummings, p. 498
3.	D	T3	Cummings, pp. 499–500
4.	D	T4	Cummings, p. 500
5.	A	T5	Cummings, p. 501
6.	B	T6	Cummings, p. 502
7.	D	T6	Cummings, p. 502
8.	A	T7	Cummings, p. 503
9.	A	T7	Cummings, p. 505
10.	C	T8	Cummings, p. 506
11.	A	T8	Cummings, p. 507
12.	B	T8	Cummings, p. 507
13.	D	V9	Video
14.	C	V10	Video
15.	A	V11	Video
16.	C	V12	Video
17.		T1	Cummings, pp. 495–497
18.		T2, T3	Cummings, pp. 498–500
19.		T5	Cummings, pp. 501–502
20.		V10	Video
21.		V11	Video
22.		V12	Video

Lesson 23

Criminal Justice

LESSON ASSIGNMENTS

Review the following assignments in order to schedule your time appropriately. Pay careful attention. The titles and numbers of the textbook chapter, the telecourse guide lesson, and the video program may be different from one another.

Text:
>Cummings and Wise, *Democracy Under Pressure*, Chapter 15, "Justice," pp. 491–494 and pp. 508–530.

Video:
>"Criminal Justice" from the series *Voices in Democracy: United States Government*.

Activities:
>One or more activities may be assigned to this lesson. Refer to your syllabus.

OVERVIEW

This lesson examines the criminal justice system of the United States. Key components and procedures of the U.S. system of law are described. We also examine recent trends in crime and evaluate the attempts that have been made to reduce crime. Criticisms of the criminal justice system are considered. Specific institutions and procedures of the criminal justice system are described and examined. The lesson also deals with the constitutionality of the death penalty. We trace the Supreme Court's ruling on the death penalty, specifically analyzing the circumstances under which the practice may be found constitutional or unconstitutional. Finally, the arguments for and against the death penalty are evaluated in light of recent evidence.

LESSON GOAL

You should be able to evaluate the effectiveness of the current justice system and identify possible alternative solutions.

TEXTBOOK OBJECTIVES

The following objectives are designed to help you get the most from the text. Review them before reading the assignment. You may want to write notes to reinforce what you have learned.

1. Define the following terms and explain their relation to the U.S. judicial system: *common law, natural law,* the *sociological school of law, stare decisis, precedent, statutory law, civil case, criminal case,* and *administrative law.*

2. Describe current trends in crime in the United States. Evaluate why the United States has such a high crime rate and why it is such a salient national issue. Discuss attempts to deal with crime and evaluate the criticisms of the criminal justice system in the United States.

3. Discuss the functions of the Justice Department and the FBI, and discuss the ways in which these institutions have been politicized.

4. Define the following terms and discuss their relationship to the U.S. criminal justice system: *adversary system of justice, plea bargaining, bail, indictment,* and *arraignment.*

5. Trace the development of the Supreme Court's rulings on the constitutionality of the death penalty. Describe recent trends about the death penalty. Evaluate the effectiveness of the death penalty as a deterrent to crime.

VIDEO OBJECTIVES

The following objectives are designed to help you get the most from the video segment of this lesson. Review them before watching the video. You may want to write notes to reinforce what you have learned.

6. Explain the effect media have on high crime rate perceptions and why "law and order" remains a controversial issue.

7. Evaluate the effectiveness of current solutions to crime. Identify possible alternative solutions.

8. Explain the continuing controversy over the use of capital punishment in the United States.

9. Explain the U.S. Supreme Court's rulings on the death penalty in *Furman v. Georgia, Gregg v. Georgia,* and *McClesky v. Kemp.*

PRACTICE TEST

After reading the assignment, watching the video, and addressing the objectives, you should be able to complete the following Practice Test. Some essay questions in this Practice Test may be included in your exams. When you have completed the Practice Test, turn to the Answer Key to score your answers.

MULTIPLE CHOICE

Select the single best answer. If more than one answer is required, it will be so indicated.

1. A body of rules that is made by government for society, interpreted by the courts, and backed by the power of the state is _____
   A. *certiorari.*
   B. law.
   C. precedent.
   D. input.

2. Which of the following justified policy on the basis of natural law?
   A. John Locke
   B. American revolutionaries
   C. Dr. Martin Luther King, Jr.
   D. All of the above

3. An action that violates a federal statute that was designed to protect the public order violates which type of law?
   A. Civil law
   B. Criminal law
   C. Natural law
   D. Administrative law

4. The crime bill enacted into law in 1994 and signed by Clinton banned how many types of semi-automatic assault weapons?
   A. Fifteen
   B. Seventeen
   C. Twenty-one
   D. Nineteen

5. According to your authors, what effect do the nation's prisons appear to have on the crime rate?
   A. They appear to lower the crime rate because most are successful in rehabilitating offenders.
   B. They contribute to the rise in the crime rate because instead of rehabilitating offenders they serve only as human warehouses for the custody of convicts.
   C. They contribute to lowering the crime rate because they act as deterrents to crime.
   D. They contribute to the rise in the crime rate because they act like the courts and coddle criminals.

6. The U.S. Justice Department is headed by _____
   A. the director of the FBI.
   B. the chief justice of the Supreme Court.
   C. the attorney general.
   D. the director of the CIA.

7. The investigative arm of the Justice Department is _____
   A. the CIA.
   B. the FBI.
   C. the NSC.
   D. the White House staff.

8. A system in which the power of the state is balanced by defendant's constitutional rights and the presumption of innocence until proven guilty is called _____
   A. the due process system.
   B. the plea bargain system.
   C. the adversary system.
   D. the common law system.

9. A person charged with a serious federal crime must first be accused in _____
   A. an indictment by a grand jury.
   B. a plea bargain arrangement.
   C. a bail bargain arrangement.
   D. an information issued by a judge.

10. According to polls, _____
    A. citizens in the United States appear to favor capital punishment.
    B. citizens in the United States overwhelmingly oppose capital punishment.
    C. citizens in the United States have no opinion regarding capital punishment.
    D. citizens favor the use of capital punishment but only by the federal courts.

11. According to Professor Zimring, California is the home of one of the nation's toughest and craziest laws, the _____
    A. "eye for an eye" law.
    B. "foul ball" law.
    C. "three strikes" law.
    D. "golden rule" law.

12. To combat violent crime, over half the states have passed "truth in sentencing" measures, which require those convicted to _____
    A. admit their guilt before being sentenced.
    B. be sentenced by their victims or the victims' families.
    C. serve at least 85 percent of their sentence.
    D. serve at least 50 percent of their sentence.

13. According to Congressman McCollum, as a result of the "truth in sentencing" measures, some states have seen a decrease in their crime rates because the criminal justice system has _____
    A. put back some deterrent effect.
    B. finally identified the revolving door syndrome.
    C. focused only on violent crimes.
    D. made violent crimes federal offenses.

14. Instead of ruling that the death penalty is cruel and unusual and therefore unconstitutional, the U.S. Supreme Court ruled that _____
    A. only heinous crimes merit the death penalty.
    B. ambiguous laws for the death penalty were unconstitutional.
    C. only murder of a minor warrants the death penalty.
    D. only specific means of the death penalty can be performed.

15. The U.S. Supreme Court decision that addressed the death penalty as it is imposed on racial minorities is _____
    A. *Miranda v. Arizona.*
    B. *Furman v. Georgia.*
    C. *Gregg v. Georgia.*
    D. *McClesky v. Kemp.*

ESSAY/PROBLEM QUESTIONS

16. Compare and contrast *natural law*, *common law*, and *sociological law*. Evaluate the appropriateness of each for a system of justice in a democratic society.

17. Define the following terms: *adversary system, plea bargaining, bail,* and *indictment*. Describe how these features are related to each other.

18. Describe the Supreme Court's position on capital punishment. Under what circumstances is the Court more likely to find the death penalty constitutional or unconstitutional? Evaluate the effectiveness of the death penalty as a deterrent to crime.

19. Explain the role that media play on perceptions of criminal activity which increases the politics of "law and order" as a controversial issue.

20. On what constitutional grounds would you support capital punishment? Oppose it? Explain your answer.

21. What are the implications of the death penalty on society? Explain the negative and positive impacts on society according to the video lesson.

ANSWER KEY

The following provides the answers and references for the Practice Test questions. Objectives are referenced using the following abbreviations:
T=Textbook Objectives   V=Video Objectives

#	Answer	Objective	Reference
1.	B	T1	Cummings, p. 493
2.	D	T1	Cummings, p. 493
3.	B	T1	Cummings, p. 493
4.	D	T2	Cummings, pp. 510–511
5.	B	T2	Cummings, p. 513
6.	C	T3	Cummings, p. 516
7.	B	T3	Cummings, p. 517
8.	C	T4	Cummings, p. 519
9.	A	T4	Cummings, p. 520
10.	A	T5	Cummings, pp. 522–523
11.	C	V6	Video
12.	C	V7	Video
13.	A	V7	Video
14.	B	V8	Video
15.	D	V9	Video
16.		T1	Cummings, pp. 493–494
17.		T4	Cummings, pp. 519–522
18.		T5	Cummings, pp. 522–525
19.		V6	Video
20.		V8	Video
21.		V8	Video

Lesson 24

Due Process of Law

LESSON ASSIGNMENTS

Review the following assignments in order to schedule your time appropriately. Pay careful attention. The titles and numbers of the textbook chapter, the telecourse guide lesson, and the video program may be different from one another.

Text:
> Cummings and Wise, *Democracy Under Pressure*, Chapter 4, "Civil Liberties and Citizenship," pp. 104–114.

Video:
> "Due Process of Law" from the series *Voices in Democracy: United States Government*.

Activities:
> One or more activities may be assigned to this lesson. Refer to your syllabus.

OVERVIEW

This lesson examines the protection of due process of law. It historically traces over time the Supreme Court's interpretation of such key protections as protection against unreasonable search and seizure, the right to counsel, and the protection against self-incrimination and double jeopardy. We also discuss how the Supreme Court has made these rights apply to the states through the Fourteenth Amendment. This lesson evaluates the way in which the Court has balanced concerns for liberty with the competing value of order and public safety. The Supreme Court has narrowed the protection of criminal rights in recent years. It is important to protect those accused of crime as they are innocent until proven guilty in an adversarial system of justice.

LESSON GOAL

You should be able to explain the role the Bill of Rights plays in guaranteeing due process of law to those accused of a crime as they go through the judicial system.

TEXTBOOK OBJECTIVES

The following objectives are designed to help you get the most from the text. Review them before reading the assignment. You may want to write notes to reinforce what you have learned.

1. Define *due process* and distinguish between substantive due process and procedural due process. Describe the Supreme Court's use of these concepts.

2. Describe the key rulings of the Supreme Court on Fourth Amendment protection against unreasonable search and seizure. Discuss the Court's decisions on the use of evidence obtained under illegal circumstances. Evaluate how well the Court has balanced order and procedural rights for criminal suspects.

3. Describe the ways in which technology has made eavesdropping on private conversations and actions easier. Discuss the government's use of wiretapping and the courts' subsequent rulings on this behavior.

4. Describe the key rights that the accused can expect to enjoy. Discuss the Supreme Court cases that have established or curbed these protections. Evaluate whether the courts have gone too far in protecting the rights of the accused.

5. Define the term *selective incorporation* and trace the incorporation of key components in the Bill of the Rights.

VIDEO OBJECTIVES

The following objectives are designed to help you get the most from the video segment of this lesson. Review them before watching the video. You may want to write notes to reinforce what you have learned.

6. Explain the role of the Bill of Rights.

7. Discuss the principles of the Fourth Amendment, especially as they apply to probable cause.

8. Discuss the provisions of the Fifth Amendment, particularly the due process clause as it applies to law enforcement.

9. Explain the effects of the Sixth Amendment on the lives of those who are accused of a crime.

10. Explain "excessive bail" and "cruel and unusual punishment" as provisions in the Eighth Amendment.

PRACTICE TEST

After reading the assignment, watching the video, and addressing the objectives, you should be able to complete the following Practice Test. Some essay questions in this Practice Test may be included in your exams. When you have completed the Practice Test, turn to the Answer Key to score your answers.

MULTIPLE CHOICE

Select the single best answer. If more than one answer is required, it will be so indicated.

1. Which of the following provides for the due process of law?
    A. The First and Second Amendments
    B. The Fifth and Fourteenth Amendments
    C. The Tenth and Thirteenth Amendments
    D. The Nineteenth and Twelfth Amendments

2. The right of an indigent person to be provided legal counsel by the state when that person is on trial for an offense that could lead to imprisonment was the result of which of the following cases?
   A. *Miranda v. Arizona*
   B. *Gideon v. Wainwright*
   C. *Roe v. Wade*
   D. *Barron v. Baltimore*

3. In deciding cases involving the protection against illegal searches and seizures, the Supreme Court has ruled that _____
   A. police may not enter a home without a warrant in order to make a routine arrest.
   B. school officials needed only "reasonable grounds" to search a student's locker.
   C. police may not ransack a home in the course of making a lawful arrest but must confine their search to the suspect and the immediate surroundings.
   D. all of the above.

4. While considering the exclusionary rule, the Supreme Court has made which of the following rulings?
   A. That the government may use illegally seized evidence in order to discredit statements made by a defendant during cross-examination at a trial
   B. That if the police were exercising "good faith" when relying on a flawed search warrant, the evidence seized could be used in court
   C. That illegally seized evidence may be admitted at a trial if the prosecution can show that the evidence would "inevitably" have been discovered by lawful means
   D. All of the above

5. A finding by a grand jury that there is enough evidence to warrant a criminal trial is known as _____
   A. a conviction.
   B. an interrogation.
   C. an arraignment.
   D. an indictment.

6. The American constitutional tradition that we do not force criminal suspects to testify against themselves or to incriminate themselves in the criminal interrogation process was upheld in the Supreme Court decision in _____
   A. *Griswold v. Connecticut.*
   B. *Miranda v. Arizona.*
   C. *Gideon v. Wainwright.*
   D. *Baker v. Carr.*

7. What did the Supreme Court do in the *Escobedo* case, the *Miranda* case, and the *Gideon* case?
   A. It strengthened the rights of persons accused of a crime.
   B. It defined and applied the freedom of expression, which is protected in the First Amendment.
   C. It defined and applied the right of privacy.
   D. It defined and applied the establishment clause.

8. In which of the following cases was the issue of double jeopardy involved?
   A. *Palko v. Connecticut*
   B. *Gideon v. Wainwright*
   C. *Benton v. Maryland*
   D. *Miranda v. Arizona*

9. Most of the provisions of the Bill of Rights are essentially _____
   A. guarantees of fiscal freedom.
   B. guarantees of authoritarian procedure.
   C. a code of criminal procedure.
   D. a code of civil procedure.

10. The Fourth Amendment was designed to be very specific to prevent _____
    A. confusion.
    B. vagueness.
    C. full-scale search.
    D. general search.

11. All of the following are rights included in the Miranda warning EXCEPT _____
    A. anything you say can and will be used against you in a court of law.
    B. you have the right to an attorney.
    C. you have the right to remain silent.
    D. anyone associated with you will also be retained.

12. Police Chief Gonzales of the Oklahoma City Police Department believes that the Miranda warning has resulted in legislation that brought about all of the following changes EXCEPT _____
    A. better press coverage.
    B. better police officers.
    C. better police training.
    D. better ability to do what the public expects.

13. The provisions in the Fifth and Sixth Amendments that protect citizens from the dangers of overzealous police and prosecutors are called the _____
    A. eminent domain clause.
    B. separation of powers clause.
    C. due process of law rights.
    D. rights of the oppressed.

14. If Congress would change the law so that there is no disparity between possession of powdered cocaine and crack cocaine, people possessing the same amount will _____
    A. receive equal compensation.
    B. get the same sentence.
    C. be tried in the same court.
    D. be imprisoned in the same state.

ESSAY/PROBLEM QUESTIONS

15. Define *due process*. Describe how substantive due process and procedural due process are different. Identify the parts of the Constitution that provide for these protections. In what areas has the Supreme Court applied these concepts?

16. On what constitutional basis is drug testing allowed? Do you favor or oppose drug testing? Why or why not? And in which situation?

17. Discuss the ways in which technology has created opportunities for the government to "overhear" conversations. Describe examples of the government's use of wiretapping and discuss the Supreme Court's ruling on the use of wiretaps. Identify which constitutional rights are at issue here.

18. You have been arrested because you are suspected to have committed a crime. List the key rights that you can expect to have and identify where they are specifically given in the Constitution.

19. How would you describe the U.S. legal system? If you were accused of a crime, what would you expect from the legal system? Describe in detail all your rights.

20. What results has the Miranda warning imposed on law enforcement? Do you favor or oppose this decision? Why or why not?

ANSWER KEY

The following provides the answers and references for the Practice Test questions. Objectives are referenced using the following abbreviations:
T=Textbook Objectives   V=Video Objectives

#	Ans	Obj	Reference
1.	B	T1	Cummings, p. 104
2.	B	T2	Cummings, p. 112
3.	D	T2	Cummings, pp. 104–108
4.	D	T2	Cummings, pp. 106–108
5.	D	T4	Cummings, p. 109
6.	B	T4, V8	Cummings, pp. 110–112, Video
7.	A	T4	Cummings, pp. 110–112
8.	A	T5	Cummings, p. 113
9.	C	V6	Video
10.	D	V7	Video
11.	D	V8	Video
12.	A	V8	Video
13.	C	V9	Video
14.	B	V10	Video
15.		T1	Cummings, pp. 104–112
16.		T2	Cummings, p. 105
17.		T3	Cummings, pp. 108–109
18.		T4	Cummings, pp. 109–112
19.		V7, V8, V9, V10	Video
20.		V8	Video

Lesson 25

First Amendment Freedoms

LESSON ASSIGNMENTS

Review the following assignments in order to schedule your time appropriately. Pay careful attention. The titles and numbers of the textbook chapter, the telecourse guide lesson, and the video program may be different from one another.

Text:
>Cummings and Wise, *Democracy Under Pressure*, Chapter 4, "Civil Liberties and Citizenship," pp. 87-104.

Video:
>"First Amendment Freedoms" from the series *Voices in Democracy: United States Government*.

Activities:
>One or more activities may be assigned to this lesson. Refer to your syllabus.

OVERVIEW

This lesson deals with the key civil liberties provided in the Constitution. In examining the religious freedoms, freedom of speech, assembly, and press, and the right to privacy, this lesson describes the way in which the Supreme Court has tried to balance constitutionally protected freedoms with society's concern for order and the welfare of the nation. You will be able to trace the development of the Supreme Court's interpretation of these freedoms and evaluate whether the Supreme Court has done a good job in balancing these competing values throughout history. Today, the courts and the Supreme Court in particular are challenged by the new electronic communications as they attempt to protect freedom of expression and balance rights of the individual including privacy.

LESSON GOAL

Describe the value of the First Amendment freedoms for democracy and explain the impact of advancing technology on the lives of today's citizens.

TEXTBOOK OBJECTIVES

The following objectives are designed to help you get the most from the text. Review them before reading the assignment. You may want to write notes to reinforce what you have learned.

1. Discuss the tension between liberty and order.

2. Describe the Bill of Rights and to whom its restrictions apply.

3. Trace the development of the Supreme Court's interpretation of the First Amendment protection of free speech. Discuss the success or failure of the Court in achieving an appropriate balance between liberty and order.

4. Describe briefly the Supreme Court's ruling on freedom of the press. When can the press be limited?

5. Trace the development of the Supreme Court's holding on obscenity in regard to First Amendment protection of free speech. Evaluate whether the Supreme Court has ruled appropriately based on the standards it has set.

6. Trace the development of the right to privacy in Supreme Court decisions and discuss Congress' efforts to protect privacy rights. Discuss how the rights of privacy may be balanced with other freedoms.

7. Discuss the Supreme Court's interpretation of freedom of assembly through its various decisions. Evaluate whether the Supreme Court has appropriately balanced liberty and order with this issue.

8. Discuss the Supreme Court's decisions on the free exercise clause and evaluate how the Court has balanced order and liberty concerns.

9. Discuss how Supreme Court decisions have dealt with the issue of separation of church and state. Discuss how the free exercise clause and establishment clause can conflict with each other.

10. Discuss past efforts to curb disloyal speech and enhance national security. Evaluate the appropriateness of these actions and of the Supreme Court's decisions on this issue.

VIDEO OBJECTIVES

The following objectives are designed to help you get the most from the video segment of this lesson. Review them before watching the video. You may want to write notes to reinforce what you have learned.

11. Describe the value of the First Amendment freedoms for democracy, focusing on freedom of the press and free speech.

12. Discuss freedom of speech and press in relation to new electronic technology.

13. Examine the right to privacy as modern technology has made possible a new form of intrusion into the private lives of individuals.

14. Explain the impact of advancing technology on the lives of today's citizens.

PRACTICE TEST

After reading the assignment, watching the video, and addressing the objectives, you should be able to complete the following Practice Test. Some essay questions in this Practice Test may be included in your exams. When you have completed the Practice Test, turn to the Answer Key to score your answers.

MULTIPLE CHOICE

Select the single best answer. If more than one answer is required, it will be so indicated.

1. The question of civil liberties has often involved _____
   A. balancing rights of many individuals.
   B. balancing liberty and order.
   C. balancing the individual's right with society's interests.
   D. all of the above.

2. Who ultimately determines how the Bill of Rights will be defined and applied?
   A. Congress
   B. The president
   C. The Supreme Court
   D. The states

3. The Court used the "clear and present danger" doctrine when deciding cases that involved which of the following?
   A. Freedom of speech
   B. Freedom of the press
   C. The right of reporters to protect the confidentiality of their sources
   D. The protection against illegal searches and seizures

4. Which of the following is NOT considered to be symbolic speech and therefore is not protected by the Constitution?
   A. Wearing black arm bands to school to protest the Vietnam War
   B. Burning one's draft card
   C. Wearing a patch of the American flag on the seat of one's blue jeans
   D. None of the above; all of them are considered to be symbolic speech by the Court

Lesson 25—First Amendment Freedoms

5. Which of the following Supreme Court justices were known to advocate the "absolute" position regarding freedom of expression?
   A. Felix Frankfurter and Robert Jackson
   B. Earl Warren and Warren Burger
   C. Hugo Black and William Douglas
   D. William Rehnquist and Antonin Scalia

6. In regard to freedom of the press, the Supreme Court has _____
   A. protected the right absolutely.
   B. balanced the right with the right to privacy.
   C. balanced the right with competing needs of society.
   D. both B and C.

7. In *Miller v. California* the Supreme Court _____
   A. ruled that the state must provide an indigent person with legal representation.
   B. ruled that a person's right to legal counsel begins prior to the time that the person appears in court.
   C. set new standards for defining obscenity.
   D. ruled that the public transporting of children to private and parochial schools does not violate the First Amendment.

8. Which of the following is not specifically provided for in the Constitution?
   A. Right of privacy
   B. Equal rights for minorities
   C. Right to vote
   D. None of the above

9. Who wrote that the framers of the Constitution sought to give Americans "the right to be let alone—the right most valued by civilized men"?
   A. Justice Oliver Wendell Holmes, Jr.
   B. Justice Louis Brandeis
   C. Justice Thurgood Marshall
   D. Justice Potter Stewart

10. The First Amendment's protection of the freedom of assembly does NOT prevent a city from passing which of the following?
    A. An ordinance that requires a permit for sound trucks, parades, and demonstrations in the interest of controlling traffic and the regulation of city streets and public parks
    B. An ordinance that prevents a march by Nazis through the streets of a predominantly Jewish community
    C. An ordinance that forbids picketing, carrying flags, and holding demonstrations on the sidewalk outside the Supreme Court building itself
    D. All of the above

11. Under the "free exercise clause," which of the following is correct?
    A. A state may not require children to salute the flag if by doing so the children would violate their religious beliefs.
    B. Both the state and federal governments have the authority to pass legislation that permits the sacramental use of some hallucinogens.
    C. The Internal Revenue Service was not in violation of this clause when it revoked the tax-exempt status of a school that practiced racial discrimination.
    D. All of the above.

12. The Supreme Court has upheld which of the following state actions as not being in violation of the establishment clause?
    A. Giving all of the state's taxpayers a tax deduction for tuition, transportation, textbooks, and other instructional costs
    B. Granting federal income tax credits and reimbursement for tuition in parochial schools
    C. Granting direct aid to church-related schools by government
    D. All of the above

13. The McCarran Act did which of the following?
    A. Granted confidentiality to reporters' sources in federal courts
    B. Required communist "front" organizations to register with the U.S. attorney general
    C. Defined obscenity for the federal courts
    D. Made it a felony to advocate the overthrow of the U.S. government by force

14. The bedrock of personal liberty in the United States is found in the _____
    A. Declaration of Independence.
    B. Articles of Confederation.
    C. First Amendment to the U.S. Constitution.
    D. Emancipation Proclamation.

15. Limitations on free speech generally have to do with speech which _____
    A. poses an immediate threat to public order.
    B. presents a constitutional question.
    C. is untrue.
    D. defames a politician's character.

16. In 1996, Congress passed legislation making it a criminal offense to knowingly transmit an obscene or indecent message to a minor; this legislation is called _____
    A. Americans with Disabilities Act.
    B. Privacy Act.
    C. Child Obscenity Act.
    D. Communications Decency Act.

17. By a unanimous vote, the Supreme Court declared the Communications Decency Act of 1996 as _____
    A. an abomination to human decency.
    B. the most advanced legislation in the 1900s.
    C. an abridgment of the First Amendment.
    D. an aberration of justice.

18. Cyberspace does not conform to traditional notions of national sovereignty, and its citizens, nicknamed _____, often perceive the Internet as a kind of country of its own.
    A. "nimbys"
    B. "pandas"
    C. "netizens"
    D. "cybizens"

19. While many are using the Internet to escape the restrictions of public space, governments and private organizations are using the same technological advances to _____
    A. collect information.
    B. restrict surveillance.
    C. recruit employees.
    D. research population growth.

20. According to many analysts, advancing computer technology is revolutionizing the way we _____
    A. learn.
    B. communicate.
    C. think.
    D. all of the above.

ESSAY/PROBLEM QUESTIONS

21. Briefly describe how the Supreme Court has arrived at its constitutional definition of the right to privacy. Include important cases in your discussion. Discuss how the rights of privacy are balanced with other freedoms.

22. Discuss the establishment clause and the free exercise clause of the First Amendment. What do they protect? Thus far, which activities has the Supreme Court protected or declined to protect under these clauses? Evaluate whether the Court has done a good job in balancing the competing values.

23. What are the "clear and present danger" and "balancing" tests? What constitutional issue is the Court attempting to define and apply? Evaluate whether the Court has done a good job in balancing the competing values.

24. How would you define "free speech" and "free press"? Do you think your definitions fall within the parameters of the Supreme Court's interpretation? Why/Why not?

25. Do you use the Internet? What restrictions, if any, do you think should be imposed on its use? Explain using the principles of free expression and privacy from this lesson.

26. Explain how modern technology has invaded our personal lives. Do you think the government and corporations should be allowed to pry into our personal lives? Why/Why not?

ANSWER KEY

The following provides the answers and references for the Practice Test questions. Objectives are referenced using the following abbreviations:
T=Textbook Objectives   V=Video Objectives

#	Ans	Obj	Reference
1.	D	T1	Cummings, pp. 89–90
2.	C	T2	Cummings, p. 90
3.	A	T3	Cummings, p. 91
4.	B	T3	Cummings, p. 91
5.	C	T3	Cummings, p. 94
6.	D	T4	Cummings, pp. 94–95
7.	C	T5	Cummings, pp. 95–96
8.	A	T6	Cummings, p. 97
9.	B	T6	Cummings, p. 97
10.	A	T7	Cummings, p. 98
11.	D	T8	Cummings, p. 99
12.	A	T9	Cummings, pp. 101–102
13.	B	T10	Cummings, p. 104
14.	C	V11	Video
15.	A	V11	Video
16.	D	V12	Video
17.	C	V12	Video
18.	C	V12	Video
19.	A	V13	Video
20.	D	V14	Video
21.		T6	Cummings, pp. 97–99
22.		T8	Cummings, pp. 99–103
23.		T10	Cummings, pp. 91–94
24.		V11	Video
25.		V12	Video
26.		V13	Video

Lesson 25—First Amendment Freedoms

Lesson 26

The Struggle for Equal Rights

LESSON ASSIGNMENTS

Review the following assignments in order to schedule your time appropriately. Pay careful attention. The titles and numbers of the textbook chapter, the telecourse guide lesson, and the video program may be different from one another.

Text:
> Cummings and Wise, *Democracy Under Pressure*, Chapter 5, "The Struggle for Equal Rights," pp. 123–166.

Video:
> "The Struggle for Equal Rights" from the series *Voices in Democracy: United States Government*.

Activities:
> One or more activities may be assigned to this lesson. Refer to your syllabus.

OVERVIEW

This lesson examines the struggles of different groups in the United States to achieve equal rights. The lesson traces the historical discrimination of such groups as Native Americans, African Americans, Hispanics, Asian Americans, women, the disabled, and homosexuals. The long-term impact of this discrimination on the social and economic status of these groups is also examined. The lesson evaluates the success of the various civil rights movements and identifies problems that are still faced by some of these groups. The lesson also evaluates the role of Congress, the president, the Supreme Court, and the states in this struggle. Key issues such as affirmative action and abortion policy are debated. Finally, the lesson examines the current status of the equality issue and takes a look at the future of the issue as well.

LESSON GOAL

You should be able to discuss the struggle to extend "unalienable rights" to people of color, women, disabled people, and homosexuals.

TEXTBOOK OBJECTIVES

The following objectives are designed to help you get the most from the text. Review them before reading the assignment. You may want to write notes to reinforce what you have learned.

1. Recognize the foundation for the use of the term *multicultural nation* and its implication for the politics of the nation. Evaluate the idea that respect for one's cultural heritage may also be divisive in a diverse nation.

2. Historically trace the relationship between Native Americans and the U.S. government, and discuss how it has affected the lives of Native Americans. Discuss contemporary social and economic problems this group experiences, and evaluate the attempts to rectify some of these problems.

3. Describe the conditions of Hispanic farm workers, and discuss the civil rights and labor movements' attempts to make life better for farm workers. Discuss the barriers that have hurt Hispanics, and evaluate Hispanics' political gains. Understand the unique relationship of Puerto Ricans with the United States.

4. Describe the controversies surrounding undocumented aliens and their children living in the United States, including the political fallout the issue has generated in the politics of the 1990s.

5. Discuss the changing roles of women in society and identify the key political issues. Evaluate the efforts to enhance equality for women—the successes and failures.

6. Discuss the traditional barriers that Americans with disabilities and homosexual Americans have faced. Evaluate the efforts to end discrimination against these two groups of citizens.

7. Discuss the origins of institutionalized racism against African Americans, and trace its progress and eventual legal demise through key Supreme Court cases.

Lesson 26—The Struggle for Equal Rights

Discuss the problems with implementing integration and the more recent controversy over busing.

8. Trace the progress of the civil rights movement over time. Identify the movements' key actors and strategies. Evaluate its effect on racism in the United States and its role in contemporary politics.

9. Identify the origins of the Civil Rights Act of 1964 and the Voting Rights Act of 1965. Identify the key factors supporting and opposing these bills. Identify and discuss the main provisions of each act, and evaluate their impact on U.S. politics.

10. Discuss the meaning of affirmative action and the Supreme Court cases which have ruled on it. Evaluate the effectiveness of affirmative action programs, and evaluate whether the need for these programs remains today.

11. Assess where we stand today in terms of equality for all groups of citizens, and evaluate the future role this issue may play in U.S. politics.

VIDEO OBJECTIVES

The following objectives are designed to help you get the most from the video segment of this lesson. Review them before watching the video. You may want to write notes to reinforce what you have learned.

12. Discuss the struggle to extend "unalienable rights" to people of color and to women.

13. Explain the difference in today's racism and the racism exhibited in the past.

14. Explain stereotyping and its effect on people of color.

15. Define *affirmative action*, and explain its effects on today's citizens. Analyze the debate for and against affirmative action.

PRACTICE TEST

After reading the assignment, watching the video, and addressing the objectives, you should be able to complete the following Practice Test. Some essay questions in this Practice Test may be included in your exams. When you have completed the Practice Test, turn to the Answer Key to score your answers.

MULTIPLE CHOICE

Select the single best answer. If more than one answer is required, it will be so indicated.

1. Which of the following statements correctly describes the citizenship of American Indians?
   A. The Supreme Court ruled in 1865 that the Fifteenth Amendment made them U.S. citizens.
   B. They have been citizens since the 1800s.
   C. Congress passed an act in 1924 to make them U.S. citizens.
   D. They are not considered citizens of the United States if they live on a reservation.

2. AIM is an organization that is interested in furthering the interests of which of the following people?
   A. African Americans
   B. American Indians
   C. Hispanics
   D. Asian Americans

3. Which of the following statements correctly describes the goals of United Farm Workers?
   A. To protect dairy prices for American farmers
   B. To provide the same rights for farm workers as union members in other industries
   C. To have legally recognized the right of farm workers to collectively organize
   D. Both B and C

4. The New Progressive Party supports which of the following positions?
   A. Statehood for Puerto Rico
   B. Independence for Puerto Rico
   C. Commonwealth status for Puerto Rico
   D. Terrorism to support Puerto Rican independence

5. Which of the following statements correctly describes Proposition 187?
   A. It was passed in 1994 by the state of California to deny welfare and other benefits to illegal immigrants.
   B. It was passed in 1994 by the state of Texas to deny welfare benefits to both legal and illegal immigrants.
   C. It was passed in 1994 by the state of Texas to deny publicly funded education to the children of illegal immigrants.
   D. It was passed in Colorado to prevent the state from banning discrimination against gays.

6. In 1996 two women associate justices, _____ and _____, sat on the Supreme Court.
   A. Sandra Day O'Connor and Diane Sterns
   B. Ruth Bader Ginsburg and Janet Reno
   C. Geraldine Ferraro and Marie Rossi
   D. Sandra Day O'Connor and Ruth Bader Ginsburg

7. Which of the following was formed to promote issues pertaining specifically to the status of women?
   A. The National Organization for Women (NOW)
   B. AIM
   C. The National Women's Political Caucus
   D. FALN

8. In 1980, a political action committee, the _____, was formed to elect officials who support gay rights.
   A. Human Rights Campaign
   B. Gay Way Campaign
   C. Gay and Lesbian Campaign
   D. Stay the Way Campaign

Lesson 26—The Struggle for Equal Rights

9. Which of the following reversed the *Dred Scott* decision?
   A. First Amendment
   B. Fourteenth Amendment
   C. Nineteenth Amendment
   D. Twenty-seventh Amendment

10. In the case of *Plessy v. Ferguson* the Supreme Court adopted which of the following?
    A. The doctrine of "separate but equal"
    B. The doctrine that segregation is "inherently unequal"
    C. The doctrine that desegregation must take place with "all deliberate speed"
    D. The doctrine that the Fourteenth Amendment forbids only discrimination by states but not discrimination by private citizens

11. In which of the following cases did the Court rule that the doctrine of "separate but equal" is unconstitutional?
    A. The *Dred Scott* case
    B. The Civil Rights Cases of 1883
    C. *Plessy v. Ferguson*
    D. *Brown v. Board of Education of Topeka, Kansas*

12. The decision of the Supreme Court in the case of *Brown v. Board of Education of Topeka, Kansas* was based on the Court's interpretation of the _____
    A. First Amendment.
    B. Tenth Amendment.
    C. Fourteenth Amendment.
    D. Twenty-seventh Amendment.

13. Which of the following used Gandhi's theory of nonviolence to further the rights of African Americans?
    A. Martin Luther King, Jr.
    B. James Meredith
    C. Stokely Carmichael
    D. Rosa Parks

14. Which of the following was a provision of the Civil Rights Act of 1964?
    A. It prohibited discrimination based upon religion or race in public accommodations that affect interstate commerce.
    B. It prohibited discrimination because of race, color, gender, religion, or national origin by employers and labor unions.
    C. It barred voting registrars from adopting different standards for white and black applicants.
    D. All of the above.

15. Your authors attribute the increase in black voter participation and the increase in the number of minority people who are now serving in public office to which of the following?
    A. The Fifteenth Amendment
    B. The Civil Rights Act of 1964
    C. The Voting Rights Act of 1965
    D. The Supreme Court decision in *Brown v. Board of Education of Topeka, Kansas*

16. In its ruling in the *Bakke* case, the Supreme Court held that _____
    A. universities have the right to give preference to blacks and other minorities as long as they do not use rigid racial "quotas."
    B. the history of the 1964 Civil Rights Act shows that it was designed to prohibit all private affirmative action programs.
    C. affirmative action plans to protect recently hired black employees must yield to seniority when layoffs are necessary.
    D. Allan Bakke had no right to be admitted to the medical school of the University of California at Davis.

17. By 2000, there were _____ African Americans in Congress and more than eight thousand black elected officials throughout the nation.
    A. twenty-five
    B. thirty
    C. forty
    D. fifty

18. Equality was envisioned by the Founders as equality among _____
    A. naturalized citizens.
    B. native-born citizens.
    C. all white citizens.
    D. white males.

19. The diverse groups of people of color and women in the United States have all the following struggles in common EXCEPT the _____
    A. experience of discrimination and prejudice.
    B. struggle against racism and sexism.
    C. persecution for their religious beliefs.
    D. struggle for equal rights.

20. According to Professor Derald Wing Sue, prejudice and racism is deeply imbedded in individuals, institutions, and in our society, and the thing that makes it so powerful is that it is _____
    A. protected in the Declaration of Independence.
    B. found throughout the world.
    C. an invisible veil.
    D. cleverly camouflaged.

21. Russell Means states that racism exists because people in the United States _____
    A. hate people who are different.
    B. learn only about family relationships.
    C. fear those they do not know.
    D. none of the above.

22. One reason that stereotypes are so damaging to racial and ethnic minorities is that they come to believe in _____
    A. themselves.
    B. the system.
    C. those stereotypes.
    D. the political leaders.

23. The attempt to correct for the historical disadvantages which women and minorities have endured was called _____
    A. due process of law.
    B. equal protection of the law.
    C. affirmative action.
    D. micro aggressions.

ESSAY/PROBLEM QUESTIONS

24. What did the Supreme Court determine when it decided the case of *Roe v. Wade*? Identify subsequent federal legislation and Supreme Court decisions that have dealt with that decision, and discuss the impact of these actions on the original ruling.

25. Discuss the key rulings in the *Dred Scott* case and in the civil rights cases of *Plessy v. Ferguson* and *Brown v. Board of Education of Topeka, Kansas*. Describe their impact on segregation. Discuss the reaction of the South to Brown and the contemporary issue of busing.

26. Define *affirmative action*. Describe the key arguments used to support and to oppose affirmative action programs. Describe how the Supreme Court has ruled on this issue.

27. Describe the irony in the struggles of women and people of color and the Declaration of Independence phrase "all men are created equal." Explain using the issues found in the video about today's world.

28. Have you ever been stereotyped? How did you feel? How do you think a lifetime of stereotyping would affect you? Do you believe that racial issues are one of the critical problems facing the United States? Why/Why not?

29. On which side of the affirmative action coin do you stand—in favor of or opposed to? Why? What do you predict will be the outcome of the affirmative action debate?

ANSWER KEY

The following provides the answers and references for the Practice Test questions. Objectives are referenced using the following abbreviations:

T=Textbook Objectives   V=Video Objectives

#	Ans	Obj	Reference
1.	C	T1	Cummings, p. 127
2.	B	T2	Cummings, p. 130
3.	D	T3	Cummings, p. 132
4.	A	T3	Cummings, p. 134
5.	A	T4	Cummings, p. 133
6.	D	T5	Cummings, p. 136
7.	A	T5	Cummings, p. 139
8.	A	T6	Cummings, p. 145
9.	B	T7	Cummings, p. 150
10.	A	T7	Cummings, p. 151
11.	D	T7	Cummings, p. 151
12.	C	T7	Cummings, p. 151
13.	A	T8	Cummings, p. 153
14.	D	T9	Cummings, pp. 155–156
15.	C	T9	Cummings, p. 157
16.	A	T10	Cummings, p. 160
17.	C	T11	Cummings, p. 161
18.	D	V12	Video
19.	C	V12	Video
20.	C	V13	Video
21.	C	V13	Video
22.	C	V14	Video
23.	C	V15	Video
24.		T5	Cummings, pp. 139–142
25.		T5	Cummings, pp. 150–151
26.		T5	Cummings, pp. 159–161
27.		V12	Video
28.		V12, V14	Video
29.		V15	Video

Contributors

We gratefully acknowledge the valuable contributions to this course from the following individuals. The titles listed were accurate when the video programs were recorded, but may have changed since the original taping.

LESSON 1—"DEMOCRATIC VOICES IN A CHANGING SOCIETY"

James Baker, Former Chief of Staff, Reagan Administration; Former Secretary of State, Reagan and Bush Administrations, Houston, TX
Larry Bartels, Professor of Politics and Public Affairs, Princeton University, Princeton, NJ
Morris Dees, Southern Poverty Law Center, Mathews, AL
Josh Dillabaugh, Foot soldier, American Indian Movement, Denver, CO
Peggy Ellis, Director of Government Affairs, CATO Institute, Washington, DC
Steve Haworth, Vice President of Public Relations, CNN News Group, Atlanta, GA
Patricia Ireland, President, National Organization for Women, Washington, DC
Russell Means, American Indian Movement, Santa Monica, CA
Francisco "Pancho" Medrano, deceased, Former UAW union organizer, Dallas, TX
Stu Mollrich, Political Consultant, Newport Beach, CA
Victor Morales, Democrat; U.S. Senatorial Candidate, Crandall, TX
Glenn Morris, Professor of Political Science, University of Colorado; Co-director, American Indian Movement of Colorado, Denver, CO
Skip Murphy, Radio Personality, KKDA-K104FM, Dallas, TX
Felice Pace, Executive Director, Klamath Forest Alliance, Etna, CA
Thomas Patterson, Professor of Government and Press, Harvard University, Cambridge, MA
Bill Price, President, Texans United for Life, Dallas, TX
Ralph Reed, Former Executive Director, Christian Coalition, Duluth, GA
Arthur Schlesinger, Jr., Presidential Scholar, City University of New York, New York, NY
David Shipler, Author of *A Country of Strangers,* Washington, DC
James Simon, Professor of Law, New York Law School, New York, NY
Derald Wing Sue, Professor of Psychology, California School of Professional Psychology, California State University, Haywood, CA
Don Thompson, Professor of Psychology, Richland College, Dallas, TX

Russell Verney, Chair, Reform Party National Committee, Dallas, TX
Jennifer Williams-Bordeaux, American Indian Movement, Denver, CO
Abigail Wright, Producer, Miranda Productions, Denver, CO
Troy Lynn Star Yellow-Wood, Denver American Indian Health Representative, American Indian Movement, Denver, CO
Bill Zimmerman, Civil Rights Activist, Santa Monica, CA

LESSON 2—"THE LIVING CONSTITUTION"

Bella Abzug, deceased, Democrat; Former Member U.S. House of Representatives from New York; Co-founder, Women's Environment and Development Organization, New York, NY
Patricia Ireland, President, National Organization for Women, Washington, DC
Susan Molinari, Republican; Former Member U.S. House of Representatives from New York, New York, NY
Glenn Morris, Professor of Political Science, University of Colorado; Co-director, American Indian Movement of Colorado, Denver, CO
David O'Brien, Professor of Government and Law, University of Virginia, Charlottesville, VA

LESSON 3—"CONSTITUTION IN CRISIS"

Melba Patillo Beal, Former student, Central High School; Member, Little Rock Nine, Little Rock, AK
Archibald Cox, Professor of Law, Harvard Law School, Cambridge, MA
Ernest Green, Former student, Central High School; Member, Little Rock Nine, Little Rock, AK
Gloria Ray Karlmark, Former student, Central High School; Member, Little Rock Nine, Little Rock, AK
Craig Rains, Former student, Central High School; Little Rock, AK
Terrence Roberts, Former student, Central High School; Member, Little Rock Nine, Little Rock, AK
Charlotte Walls La Nier, Former student, Central High School; Member, Little Rock Nine, Little Rock, AK

LESSON 4—"FEDERALISM"

Michael Cox, Texas Department of Public Safety, Austin, TX
Michael Fix, Director of Immigrant Policy, Urban Institute, Washington, DC
Jacqueline Gillian, Advocates for Auto and Highway Safety, Washington, DC
Rudolph Giuliani, Mayor, New York City, New York, NY
Sam Gonzales, Oklahoma City Police Chief, Oklahoma City, OK
Dr. Paul Heath, Bombing victim, Oklahoma City, OK
Donald Huddle, Professor of Economics, Rice University, Houston, TX
Kay Bailey Hutchison, Republican Senator from Texas, Washington, DC
Frank Keating, Governor of Oklahoma, Oklahoma City, OK
John Kincaid, Professor of Government and Law, Lafayette College, Easton, PA
Robert H. Macy, District Attorney, Oklahoma County, Oklahoma City, OK
Ron Norick, Mayor of Oklahoma City, Oklahoma City, OK
Bob Ricks, Former Special Agent in Charge, Federal Bureau of Investigation, Oklahoma City, OK
Max Sandlin, Democrat; Member U.S. House of Representatives from Texas, Washington, DC

LESSON 5—"INTERGOVERNMENTAL RELATIONS"

Patsy Bowers, Zone Manager, Lockheed Martin IMS, Miami, FL
Annette Haynes, Former participant, "YW Works", Milwaukee, WI
Theresa Johnson, Former WAGES participant, Department of Children and Families, Miami, FL
John Kincaid, Professor of Government and Law, Lafayette College, Easton, PA
Daniella Levine, Executive Director, Human Services Coalition, Miami, FL
Elaine Maly, Chief Development and Marketing Officer, YWCA of Greater Milwaukee, Milwaukee, WI
John Norquist, Mayor, Milwaukee, WI
Richard Oulahan, Executive Director, Esperanza Unida Incorporated, Milwaukee, WI
Robin Reiter, Co-chair, Dade-Monroe WAGES Coalition, Miami, FL
Antonio Riley, Member Wisconsin State House of Representatives, Madison, WI
Theresa Rozeniak, Former participant, "Wisconsin Works", Milkwaukee, WI
Rose M. Sickles, Homemaker, Welfare Recipient, Miami, FL
William M. Stokes, Project Manager, Lockheed Martin IMS, Miami, FL

Tommy Thompson, Former Governor of Wisconsin; Secretary of Health and Human Resources, Washington, DC
Don Winstead, Welfare Reform Administrator, State of Florida, Tallahassee, FL

LESSON 6—"PUBLIC OPINION AND POLITICAL SOCIALIZATION"

Laura Compton, Rumsey Hall, Washington Depot, CT
Ali Frankel, Rumsey Hall, Washington Depot, CT
Jewelle Taylor Gibbs, Professor of Sociology, University of California—Berkeley; Author, *Race and Justice*, Berkeley, CA
Denise Juarez, Newtown High School, Queens, NY
Lucy Luis, Green Park Elementary School, Walla Walla, WA
Ashok K. Mago, Chairman/President, Mago & Associates, Dallas, TX
Francisco "Pancho" Medrano, deceased, Former UAW union organizer, Dallas, TX
Gerardo Moreno, Green Park Elementary School, Walla Walla, WA
Dorothy Novilus, Rumsey Hall, Washington Depot, CT
Jonathan Rivera, Newtown High School, Queens, NY
Steve Seguis, Newtown High School, Queens, NY
Yana Sheftalovich, Newtown High School, Queens, NY
Thomas "T. J." Suckow, Green Park Elementary School, Walla Walla, WA
Nolte White, Rumsey Hall, Washington Depot, CT
Abigail Wright, Producer, Miranda Productions, Denver, CO
Michael Yetemian, Newtown High School, Queens, NY

LESSON 7—"PARTICIPATION IN DEMOCRACY"

Lily Archambault Boyce, Community member, American Indian Movement, Denver, CO
Randi Brauiroff, Glaucoma patient, Los Angeles Cannabis Buyers' Co-op, Los Angeles, CA
Steve M. Corehand, Cancer patient, Los Angeles Cannabis Buyers' Co-op, Los Angeles, CA
Josh Dillabaugh, Foot soldier, American Indian Movement, Denver, CO
Richard Eastman, AIDS patient, Vice President, Los Angeles Cannabis Buyers' Co-op, Los Angeles, CA

Scott Imler, President/Director, Los Angeles Cannabis Buyers' Co-op, Los Angeles, CA
Loma Martin, Red Horse Woman, American Indian Movement, Denver, CO
Michael Meyers, M.D., Director of Chemical Dependency Department, Cedars-Sinai Medical Center, Los Angeles, CA
Stu Mollrich, Ford & Mollrich Political Consulting Firm, Newport Beach, CA (against Proposition 215)
Glenn Morris, American Indian Movement, Boulder, CO
Jennifer Williams-Bordeaux, Community member, American Indian Movement, Denver, CO
Troy Lynn Star Yellow-Wood, Denver American Indian Health Representative, American Indian Movement, Denver, CO
Bill Zimmerman, Director, Americans for Medical Rights, Santa Monica, CA (for Proposition 215)

LESSON 8—"MASS MEDIA AND GOVERNMENT"

Ann Compton, White House Correspondent, ABC News, Washington, DC
Marlin Fitzwater, White House Press Secretary, Reagan and Bush Administrations, Washington, DC
Ed Fouhy, Former Saigon Bureau Chief, CBS News, Washington, DC
Jerry Friedheim, Former Defense Department Spokesman, Arlington, VA
Jim Fry, News reporter, WFAA-TV News, Washington, DC
Carl Leubsdorf, Washington Bureau Chief, *Dallas Morning News*, Washington, DC
Scott Pelley, Correspondent, CBS News, Washington, DC
Bill Plante, White House Correspondent, CBS News, Washington, DC

LESSON 9—"INTEREST GROUPS"

Gerald Bendix, President, Hi-Ridge Lumber Company, Yreka, CA
Peggy Ellis, Director of Government Affairs, CATO Institute, Washington, DC
John Leary, Director of Forest Issues, Sierra Club, Washington, DC
John McCain, Republican Senator from Arizona, Washington, DC
Mitch McConnell, Republican Senator from Kentucky, Washington, DC
Tanya Metaksa, Executive Director, National Rifle Association for Legislative Action, Washington, DC

Laura Murphy, Director, American Civil Liberties Union, Washington, DC
Felice Pace, Executive Director, Klamath Forest Alliance, Etna, CA
Luke Popovich, American Forest & Paper Association, Washington, DC
Donald Simon, Executive Vice President, Common Cause, Washington, DC

LESSON 10—"POLITICAL PARTIES"

Delmarie Cobb, Democratic Political Consultant, Cook County, IL
Thomas Lyons, Democratic Party Chair, Cook County, IL
Jim Nicholson, Chair, Republican National Committee, Washington, DC
Tom Pauken, Republican Party Chair, State of Texas, Dallas, TX
Bill Price, President, Texans United for Life; Republican Party Activist, Dallas, TX
Roy Romer, Former Democratic Party National Chair, Washington, DC; Governor of Colorado, Denver, CO
Russell Verney, Chair, Reform Party National Committee, Dallas, TX

LESSON 11—"MEDIA AND ELECTIONS"

Hal Bruno, Political Director, ABC News, Washington, DC
Ann Compton, White House Correspondent, ABC News, Washington, DC
Jim Fry, WFAA-TV News, Washington, DC
Kathleen Hall Jamison, Dean, Annenberg School of Communications, University of Pennsylvania, Philadelphia, PA
Carl Leubsdorf, Washington Bureau Chief, *Dallas Morning News*, Washington, DC
Thomas Patterson, Bradley Professor of Government and Press, Kennedy School of Government, Harvard University, Cambridge, MA
Bill Plante, White House Correspondent, CBS News, Washington, DC
Karl Rove, Assistant to President Bush, Washington, DC; Former Political Consultant, Austin, TX
Russell Verney, Perot Campaign Manager, Reform Party, Dallas, TX

LESSON 12—"PRESIDENTIAL ELECTIONS"

Larry Bartels, Professor of Politics and Public Affairs, Princeton University, Princeton, NJ
Ed Fouhy, Executive Producer, Presidential Debates 1988 and 1992, Washington, DC
Russell Verney, Perot Campaign Manager, Reform Party, Dallas, TX

LESSON 13—"CONGRESSIONAL ELECTIONS"

Anthony Bell, Jackson Assistant Campaign Manager, Chicago, IL
Phil Gramm, Republican Senator from Texas, Washington, DC
Rick Hill, Republican; Former Member U.S. House of Representatives from Montana, Helena, MT
Jesse Jackson, Jr., Democrat; Member U.S. House of Representatives from Illinois, Washington, DC
Joe Lamson, Yellowtail Campaign Manager, Helena, MT
Victor Morales, Democrat; U.S. Senatorial Candidate, Crandall, TX
Charmaine Murphy, Hill Campaign Manager, Helena, MT
David Orr, Chairperson, Voter Moter, Cook County Clerk, Chicago, IL
Phil Seib, Political Analyst; Professor, Southern Methodist University, Dallas, TX
Alice Tregay, Jackson Campaign Manager, Chicago, IL
Bill Yellowtail, Democrat; U.S. House of Representatives Candidate, Helena, MT

LESSON 14—"CONGRESS"

Tom DeLay, Republican; Member U.S. House of Representatives from Texas, Washington, DC
Daniel Inouye, Democratic Senator from Hawaii, Washington, DC
Loretta Sanchez, Democrat; Member U.S. House of Representatives from California, Washington, DC
J. C. Watts, Republican; Member U.S. House of Representatives from Oklahoma, Washington, DC

LESSON 15—"LEGISLATIVE PROCESS"

Mark Buse, Policy Director, U.S. Senate Commerce Committee, Washington, DC
Marie Carbone, Handgun Control, Washington, DC
Tom DeLay, Republican; Member U.S. House of Representatives from Texas, Washington, DC
Daniel Freeman, Counsel and Parliamentarian of the Judiciary Committee, U.S. House of Representatives, Washington, DC
John McCain, Republican Senator from Arizona, Washington, DC
Mitch McConnell, Republican Senator from Kentucky, Washington, DC
Tanya K. Metaksa, National Rifle Association, Washington, DC
Norman Ornstein, Resident Scholar, American Enterprise Institute, Washington, DC
Russ Verney, Former National Reform Party Chair, Dallas, TX

LESSON 16—"CONGRESS AND THE PRESIDENT"

Dan Error, Former Director of Health Resources, Health Resources and Services Administration, Garland, TX
Kay Bailey Hutchison, Republican Senator from Texas, Washington, DC
Norman Ornstein, Resident Scholar, American Enterprise Institute, Washington, DC

LESSON 17—"THE PRESIDENCY"

James Baker, Former Chief of Staff, Reagan Administration; Former Secretary of State, Reagan and Bush Administrations, Houston, TX
Thomas E. Cronin, President, Whitman College; Author, *The Paradoxes of the American Presidency*, Walla Walla, WA
Marlin Fitzwater, Former Press Secretary, Reagan Administration, Washington, DC
Jody Powell, Former Press Secretary, Carter Administration, Washington, DC
Arthur M. Schlesinger, Professor of History, City College of New York; Author, *The Imperial Presidency*, New York, NY

LESSON 18—"BUREAUCRACY"

Daniel Inouye, Democratic Senator from Hawaii, Washington, DC
Edward Lessard, Deputy Regional Administrator, Health Care Financing Administration, Dallas, TX
John McCain, Republican Senator from Arizona, Washington, DC
Stan Soloway, Assistant Undersecretary of Defense for Acquisitions and Technology, Department of Defense, Washington, DC
Bob Stone, Director, National Performance Review Committee, National Partnership for Reinventing Government, Washington, DC
Barry Valentine, Deputy Administrator, Federal Aviation Administration, Washington, DC

LESSON 19—"DOMESTIC POLICY"

Raymond Chrétien, Canada's Ambassador to the U.S., Washington, DC
Keith Collins, Chief Economist, U.S. Department of Agriculture, Washington, DC
Charles Conner, President, Corn Refiners Association; Former staff member on Agriculture Committee, Washington, DC
Sarah Fox, Member, U.S. National Labor Relations Board, Washington, DC
Rodney M. Fujita, Senior Specialist for the Environmental Defense Fund, Oakland, CA
Joe Gunn, President, Texas AFL-CIO, Austin, TX
R. Bruce Josten, Executive Vice President for Government Affairs, U.S. Chamber of Commerce, Washington, DC
Karen Kinstetter, Dead End Dairy Farm, Kewannee, WI
Dave Lehman, Group Manager Commodity Products, Chicago Board of Trade, Chicago, IL
Russell Stoer, Stoer Dairy Farm, Two Rivers, WI
Bill Woolf, Legislative Assistant to Frank Murkowski, Republican U.S. Senator from Alaska, Washington, DC

LESSON 20—"FOREIGN POLICY"

James Baker, Former Chief of Staff, Reagan Administration; Former Secretary of State, Reagan and Bush Administrations, Houston, TX
Raymond Chrétien, Canada's Ambassador to the United States, Washington, DC
Chester Crocker, Professor of Political Science, Georgetown University, Washington, DC
Ninoska Perez, Spokesperson, Cuban American National Foundation, Miami, FL

LESSON 21—"GLOBAL POLITICS"

Celso Amorim, Brazil's Ambassador to the United Nations, New York, NY
Chester Crocker, Professor of Political Science, Georgetown University; U.S. Institute of Peace, Washington, DC
Stephen Guisinger, Professor of Economics, University of Texas at Dallas, Dallas, TX
Mona Hamman, United Nations World Food Program, New York, NY
Robert Pastor, Director, Latin American Program, Carter Center, Atlanta, GA
Bill Richardson, Former U.S. Ambassador to the United Nations, Washington, DC
Gillian Sorenson, Assistant Secretary General, United Nations, New York, NY
Elsa Stamatopoulou, United Nations High Commissioner for Human Rights, New York, NY

LESSON 22—"FEDERAL COURTS"

Lawrence Baum, Professor of Political Science, Ohio State University, Columbus, OH
Elizabeth Birch, Executive Director, Human Rights Campaign, Washington, DC
Tom DeLay, Republican; Member U.S. House of Representatives from Texas, Washington, DC
Pauline Dixon, Democrat; Precinct Chair, Hamilton Park, Dallas, TX
Eddie Bernice Johnson, Democrat; Member U.S. House of Representatives from Texas, Washington, DC
Steven McFarland, Christian Legal Society, Annandale, VA
James Simon, Professor of Law, New York Law School, New York, NY
Nina Totenberg, Legal Affairs Correspondent, National Public Radio, Washington, DC

LESSON 23—"CRIMINAL JUSTICE"

James Beathard, Death Row inmate, State Penitentiary, Huntsville, TX
Tim Boutz, Director of Education, State Penitentiary, Walla Walla, WA
John Cockrum, Death Row inmate, State Penitentiary, Huntsville, TX
Lawrence Friedman, Marion Rice Firkwood Professor of Law, Stanford University, Stanford, CA
Steven Hawkins, Executive Director, National Coalition to Abolish the Death Penalty, Washington, DC
David Hillyard, Recreation Director, State Penitentiary, Walla Walla, WA
Robert H. Macy, District Attorney for Oklahoma County, Oklahoma City, OK
Dudley C. Sharp, III, Vice President, Justice for All, Houston, TX
Franklin Zimring, Director of the Earl Warren Legal Institute, University of California—Berkeley, Berkeley, CA

LESSON 24—"DUE PROCESS OF LAW"

Joyce Ann Brown, Author, *Justice Denied*, Dallas, TX
Lawrence M. Friedman, Marlon Rice Firkwood Professor of Law, Stanford University, Stanford, CA
Jewelle Taylor Gibbs, Professor of Sociology, University of California—Berkeley; Author, *Race and Justice*, Berkeley, CA
Sam Gonzales, Oklahoma City Police Chief, Oklahoma City, OK
Kimi King, Assistant Professor of Political Science, University of North Texas, Denton, TX
David O'Brien, Professor of Government and Law, University of Virginia, Charlottesville, VA
Franklin Zimring, Director of the Earl Warren Legal Institute, University of California—Berkeley, Berkeley, CA

LESSON 25—"FIRST AMENDMENT FREEDOMS"

Ann Beeson, National Staff Attorney, American Civil Liberties Union, New York, NY
Esther Dyson, Chairman, Edventure Holdings Inc., New York, NY
Lino Graglia, Professor, University of Texas School of Law, Austin, TX
Donna Rice Hughes, Communications Director, Enough is Enough, Washington, DC

LESSON 26—"THE STRUGGLE FOR EQUAL RIGHTS"

Morris Dees, Southern Poverty Law Center, Mathews, AL
Dr. Michael S. Greve, Executive Director, Center for Individual Rights, Washington, DC
Lino Graglia, Professor, University of Texas School of Law, Austin, TX
Lani Guinier, Professor of Law, Harvard Law School, Cambridge, MA
Patricia Ireland, President, National Organization for Women, Washington, DC
Ron Kirk, Mayor of Dallas, Dallas, TX
Carl Livingston, Professor of Political Science, Seattle Central Community College, Seattle, WA
Russell Means, American Indian Movement, Denver, CO
Dr. Guadalupe Quintanilla, University of Houston, Houston, TX
Gilda Sheppard, Professor of Sociology, Seattle Central Community College, Seattle, WA
David Shipler, Author, *A Country of Strangers*, Washington, DC
Derald Wing Sue, Professor of Psychology, California School of Professional Psychology, California State University, Haywood, CA